The Missionary Journeys of Paul

Dr. Dan S. Bailey

ISBN: 9798874086947
Self Published

DEDICATION

Dedicated to my Savior, the Lord Jesus Christ and to all who love Him and
are trying to reach others for Him.

Missionary Journeys of Paul (A Study in Missions)

INTRODUCTION TO MISSIONS

It is so important for the church to understand what place missions has in its existence. Missions is so important that no church should be without a good mission program being established within it. A church that is not supporting missions is a church that is not fulfilling what is at the very heart of God.

Mark 16:15 says, "And he said unto them, Go ye into all the world and preach the gospel to every creature."

Matthew 28:19 says, "Go ye therefore, and teach all nations, baptizing them in the name of the Father, and of the Son, and of the Holy Ghost:"

Acts 13:47 says, "For so hath the Lord commanded us, saying, I have set thee to be a light of the Gentiles, that thou shouldest be for salvation unto the ends of the earth."

We are commissioned by the Lord to go and tell the world about the gospel. We must be involved in this ministry for all the world deserves to hear at least one time in their lives a clear presentation of the Gospel message.

I want to show you from the Word of God what missions really is and how important it is in the life of every believer in the church and show you what God expects you to do in reaching the lost world with the message of Jesus Christ.

When you think of the words missions or missionary what is the first thing that comes to your mind? Usually you picture someone who has been sent, telling the gospel message to some lost person or people. We could see a picture in our minds of a distant remote village and a man with a Bible preaching the gospel to them. I had the privilege many years ago to go on several mission trips to Haiti and I saw first-hand what many missionaries have to face in a third world country. We went from village to village preaching and telling others about Jesus. We saw many saved in those trips, but the most eye-opening thing that I witnessed was that when someone was willing to preach the gospel many with open heart would listen and receive the message.

Romans 10:14 says, "How then shall they call on him in whom they have not believed? and how shall they believe in him of whom they have not heard? and how shall they hear without a preacher?"

Noah Webster's 1828 dictionary tells us that "mission" is from a Latin word meaning to send. He defines mission as a sending or being sent, usually the latter. "How shall they hear without a preacher?" Someone must go! Someone must tell them!

We should want to be involved in missions first of all, because He commendeth His love toward us.
"But God commendeth his love toward us, in that, while we were yet sinners, Christ died for us." Romans 5:8. Then secondly, because we are commissioned as believers to do so. *"Go ye therefore, and teach all nations, baptizing them in the name of the Father, and of the Son, and of the Holy Ghost:"* Matthew 28:19.

Alban Douglas said, "All believers are, or ought to be, constrained by the love of Jesus Christ to serve Him from conversion to death or the rapture. . . Constrained means to compel, to impel, to drive forward. In the Old Testament men were compelled by law and in the New Testament we are compelled by love. . . The life of service is an unselfish life, not serving self, but serving others. The happiest life is an unselfish life. The selfish individual is a miserable creature, always jealous lest others get more gifts or praise."

God has sent us to carry the gospel message to a lost and dying world. You may not be a preacher, but if you are saved, you are a "reacher", and you should be reaching souls for the Lord. All of God's children have this call or commission on their lives. For many God calls and sends them to a particular place to tell people about Jesus, but for others we just tell those that we can, while we can, where we are!

The words to a precious song entitled, "People Need The Lord" should encourage you to want to go. "Every day they pass me by, I can see it in their eyes. Empty people filled with care, Headed who knows where? On they go through private pain, Living fear to fear. Laughter hides their silent cries, Only Jesus hears.

People need the Lord. People need the Lord. At the end of broken dreams, He's the open door. People need the Lord. People need the Lord. When will we realize, People need the Lord?

We are called to take His light, To a world where wrong seems right. What could be too great a cost, For sharing life with one who's lost? Through His love our hearts can feel, All the grief they bear. They must hear the words of life, Only we can share.

People need the Lord. People need the Lord. At the end of broken dreams, He's the open door. People need the Lord. People need the Lord. When will we realize, That we must give our lives, For people need the Lord."

A vast majority of the world are still lost and need a Savior. Someone must tell them. Will you go? Will you tell them? Eternity depends on your choice!

PAUL'S TESTIMONY

Paul had an experience that completely changed his life. He was a religious man who was zealous in his faith. He was persecuting the Christians because he thought that it was pleasing to God. But on the Damascus Road, he came face to face with the Lord Jesus Christ. After this experience he was never the same. He wanted to tell others what happened to him. He was excited about the change and thrilled to be able to share with them what Jesus had done in his life. Do you have a testimony like that today?

Let's look at what happened in Acts 9. Verses one and two tell us that Saul was going to persecute and imprison those who were Christians. As he came near to Damascus, verse 3 says that "suddenly there shined round about him a light from Heaven."

In Chapter 7 of Acts we are told of Stephen being martyred and stoned to death. Those who were stoning him laid their coats down at the feet of a young man by the name of Saul. This is the first mention of Saul, later to be Paul, in the Scriptures. He was completely against what Christians were doing and requested here by the high priest, in Chapter 9 to be given permission to further persecute these Christians wherever he found them. The high priest gave the desired letters and Paul set out for Damascus, Syria. Little did he know that God had his hand on him and had a special plan for him.

Dr. Sightler said, "The Lord God still sits upon a throne of

His majestic glory. The reigns of the universe are yet in the hands of the Almighty. . .and shall always be in the hands of the Almighty God. . . My God is a great God and can do whatever He wills, whenever He will, and to whom He may will."

In Verse 3, we see Paul was going from Jerusalem to Damascus, which is a long journey. As he began to draw near to Damascus, Acts 9:3 says, "*And as he journeyed, he came near Damascus: and suddenly there shined round about him a light from heaven:*" Verse 4-7 says, "*And he fell to the earth, and heard a voice saying unto him, Saul, Saul, why persecutest thou me? 5 And he said, Who art thou, Lord? And the Lord said, I am Jesus whom thou persecutest: it is hard for thee to kick against the pricks. 6 And he trembling and astonished said, Lord, what wilt thou have me to do? And the Lord said unto him, Arise, and go into the city, and it shall be told thee what thou must do. 7 And the men which journeyed with him stood speechless, hearing a voice, but seeing no man.*"

No doubt from what is described here, we can say that it is in an unusual conversion experience. Most of us will not be able to relate to such an experience when we got saved. Dr. Sightler reminds us "Men are not saved, and I want you to get what I am about to say; men are not saved by experience, but men are saved by grace through faith in the Lord Jesus Christ: and experience is the result of having been saved by the grace of God."

First there was a great light shining. Then there was the voice of the Lord speaking to Saul. Verse 17 of this chapter seems to indicate that the bright shining light that Saul saw was Jesus. Matthew Henry says that Christ's manifestations of himself to poor souls are humbling; they lay them very low, in mean thoughts of themselves and a humble submission to the will of God. Now mine eyes see thee, saith

Job, I abhor myself. I saw the Lord, saith Isaiah, sitting upon a throne, and I said, Woe is me, for I am undone . . . Those whom God will employ are first struck with a sense of their unworthiness to be employed.

The Lord ask him the question, "Why persecutest thou me?" And immediately Saul as "Who are thou, Lord?" To which the Lord answers, "I am Jesus whom thou persecutest." Saul is bowing with face to the ground to the One he is persecuting. The One that he seemingly, despises the most. The Jesus that all the Christians are following and the Jesus that has a purpose for Saul. He tells him that "it is hard for thee to kick against the pricks" which implies someone who is resisting and in the process of hitting a sharp object. What the Lord is telling Saul here implies that he was only hurting himself in his effort to eliminate Christians. Saul was suffering in the process he was involved in trying to get rid of all the Christians.

Then notice the surrender of Saul, "*And he trembling and astonished said, Lord, what wilt thou have me to do?*" He trembled under strong conviction. He was astonished or filled with amazement at what the Lord was doing! Matthew Henry says "The convincing, converting, work of Christ is astonishing to the awakened soul, and fills it with admiration. He immediately cries out, "*Lord, what wilt thou have me to do?*" A moment ago, a persecutor of the Christians, and now asking Christ to instruct him into what He would have him do. Henry says, the great change in conversion is wrought upon the will, and consists in the resignation of that to the will of Christ.

The instructions that the Lord gives him is to "*Arise, and go into the city, and it shall be told thee what thou must do.*" He is encouraged that with these instructions that further instructions will follow.

Some debate the time when Saul actually got saved either on the Damascus Road or later at the house of Ananias, a certain disciple who lived in Damascus. Dr. Sightler said concerning this that as far as he is concerned, it he was converted on the Damascus Road. He says, "Paul is converted at this point, miraculously and gloriously converted with an experience unparalleled by any other personality as far as I am able to discern in all the Holy Scriptures and paralleled by only a few people in all the history of the church. . . I want to say to you whatever the need might be to get a man to his knees and to a personal faith in the Lord Jesus, God is able to produce those circumstances and to bring such people to their knees in faith and in a genuine conversion experience.
God is able, and the Lord brings Saul of Tarsus to a real experience of the grace of God so profound and so revolutionary and so changing him inwardly and outwardly that none of us have the remotest doubt but that Paul indeed is God's apostle and God's servant of renown, chosen vessel as Paul calls himself later on in his epistles.

SENT OUT

The best way to understand what missions is all about is to take a missionary trip. That's what we plan to do in these lessons on Missions. We are going to go on three missionary journeys with possibly the greatest missionary that ever lived, Paul. Pack your bags and get out your Bible and we will begin this journey.

Over the course of his ministry, the Apostle Paul traveled more than 10,000 miles and established at least 14 churches. As we follow the footsteps of Paul, we will learn the ups and downs of being a missionary as well as the great joy of doing what God calls us to do.

7

There are two cities that are called Antioch in these Scriptures. They both were named after Antiochus, father of Seleucid I. The Antioch in Acts 13 was the third largest city in ancient Rome and capital of the province of Syria. Today, it is part of southern Turkey. The *other* Antioch was part of Pisidia, an ancient region which is also now part of Turkey. It is always referred to as Antioch of Pisidia.

"Now there were in the church that was at Antioch certain prophets and teachers; as Barnabas, and Simeon that was called Niger, and Lucius of Cyrene, and Manaen, which had been brought up with Herod the tetrarch, and Saul. 2 As they ministered to the Lord, and fasted, the Holy Ghost said, Separate me Barnabas and Saul for the work whereunto I have called them." Acts 13:1-2

Acts 13:2 tells us that the first missionaries that were sent out by the church were Barnabas and Saul. "As they ministered to the Lord, and fasted, the Holy Ghost said, Separate me Barnabas and Saul for the work whereunto I have called them." We see a number of things here that we need to address concerning our understanding of missions in the church today.

First, they were sent out by the church. Verse one tells us that they were "in the church that was at Antioch". It is the responsibility of the church to send forth missionaries into the mission fields of the world today. Again verse two says they were instructed to send them because the Holy Spirit spoke to the church and told them to.

Secondly, these men had a calling on their lives. The Holy Ghost said . . . "for the work whereunto I have called them." There must be a call of God on the life of the missionary in order for them to be sent to a field. God may nudge the heart of those He wants in missions today by a burden to reach a particular group of people or to a particular country to minister in. However, every missionary that is called by God must first have a burden for the lost. If a believer is not willing to win souls here in America, they won't be of much good winning souls in a foreign land.

The Bible gives several examples of a calling of God being given to men. When the Lord called Abraham in Genesis 12:3 He said, "And in thee shall all the families of the earth be blessed." God has a divine purpose in mind when He calls an individual. Before God gave the Ten Commandments to the children of Israel in Exodus 20, in chapter 19 He said to Israel, "And ye shall be unto me a kingdom of priests, and an holy nation. These are the words which thou shalt speak unto the children of Israel."

What is meant by a kingdom of priests? Criswell says that a priest is someone who represents a man to God and God to man. Before God gave His oracles into the hands of Israel, He first said to them, "You are to be the teachers, the ambassadors, the missionaries, and the evangelists of the Word of God to all the earth." God gave the oracles from His hand and Israel was to teach them to all the nations of the world. (Criswell, pp. 123, 124)

In the Gospels of Matthew, Mark, Luke and John the story ends with the Great Commission. "*Go ye therefore, and teach all nations, baptizing them in the name of the Father, and of the Son, and of the Holy Ghost*" Matt. 28:19. Acts 1:8 says, "*Ye shall be witnesses unto me both in Jerusalem, and in all Judaea, and in Samaria, and unto the uttermost part of the earth.*" Criswell says "This is the divine mine of God." The church is set apart in the world for one great, divine purpose, namely, the conversion of the world to Jesus Christ. (*Criswell*)

William Carey was a young man in who lived in England in the late 1780s. He was obsessed with the conviction that the church must take God's Word to every nation. Carey kept urging his fellow pastors to set up a missionary agency, but they always seemed to have more urgent problems closer to home. At one meeting an elder pastor reportedly snapped at him: "Young man, sit down. When God pleases to convert the heathen, he'll do it without consulting you or me."

But this did not satisfy William Carey. He was determined not to let anything stand in his way of getting the gospel message out. Carey never went to school after the age of 12, but became a cobbler's apprentice. Because of his lack of education, he was disqualified for mission work. But he knew that God had given him abilities in languages and a burden to tell others about Jesus.

In a book that he had written in 1792, Carey showed that if Christians want to claim the comforts and promises of the New Testament, they must also accept the commands and instructions given there. It was not long after his book was published that he preached a sermon where he admonished Christian leaders to "expect great things from God; attempt great things for God." Soon afterward his colleagues formed a missionary society and sent Carey as their first missionary to India, along with a Dr. John Thomas.

William Carey spent seven years in India before seeing his first convert. Much suffering and anguish he and his family had to face, but they stuck it out. Was it worth it? With all of the things he accomplished in India, we also see that William Carey's life inspired tens of thousands to give themselves for the spread of the Gospel.
(https://www.christianity.com/church/church-history/timeline/1701-1800/william-careys-amazing-mission-11630319.html)

So many examples of those who were willing to go and to give their all for the cause of Christ in trying, with all their hearts, to win souls to Christ.

Beginning The First Missionary Journey

In Acts 13:3-4 we are told, *"And when they had fasted and prayed, and laid their hands on them, they sent them away. 4 So they, being sent forth by the Holy Ghost, departed unto Seleucia; and from thence they sailed to Cyprus."*

This is the sending forth of the first Christian foreign missionaries. Harold Willmington tells us that the church at Antioch was totally independent of the Jerusalem church and recognized no ecclesiastical hierarchy whatsoever. The cooperation that is seen here is between the church and the Holy Spirit.

Dr. Harold Sightler says in his book on Acts, "the very foundation of all mission activity down through all the years, until this day is the local church congregation . . . all the missionaries are recruited from the local church . . . the praying for the missionaries is done for the most part by the local church, and this is exactly as it ought to be. He tells us to not forget that, "this chapter records the record of the first local church which ever assumed the responsibility and the burden of getting the Gospel out through missionaries to regions beyond."(Sightler, pp. 203, 204)

And so the journey begins. Called by God, sent out by the church, the Holy Spirit continues to lead them to where He wants them to be. This missionary journey took place around A.D. 45. They left Antioch and went down to Selucia which is the port city of Antioch, about fifteen miles away.

From here they set sail for Cyprus and began their ministry there. One thing to note about the island of Cyprus is that it was Barnabas's native country. (Acts 4:36)

In verse 5 we see them preaching the word of God in the synagogues of the Jews at Salamis. John Mark was there to help in the ministry, being a part of Paul and Barnabas's team.

They first came to Seleucia which was the sea-port town opposite to Cyprus, then sailed across the sea to Cyprus. On the island of Cyprus the first city they came to was Salamis, on the east side. They preached and sowed seed here and then continued on to the city of Paphos, which is on the western coast of Cyprus.

One of the first things that they faced in their missionary journey, seen in verses 6 through 13, is opposition and discouragement.

"And when they had gone through the isle unto Paphos, they found a certain sorcerer, a false prophet, a Jew, whose name was Barjesus: 7 Which was with the deputy of the country, Sergius Paulus, a prudent man; who called for Barnabas and Saul, and desired to hear the word of God. 8 But Elymas the sorcerer (for so is his name by interpretation) withstood them, seeking to turn away the deputy from the faith. 9 Then Saul, (who also is called Paul,) filled with the Holy Ghost, set his eyes on him, 10 And said, O full of all subtilty and all mischief, thou child of the devil, thou enemy of all righteousness, wilt thou not cease to pervert the right ways of the Lord? 11 And now, behold, the hand of the Lord is upon thee, and thou shalt be blind, not seeing the sun for a season. And immediately there fell on him a mist and a darkness; and he went about seeking some to lead him by the hand. 12 Then the deputy, when he saw what was done, believed, being astonished at the doctrine of the Lord. 13 Now when Paul and his company

loosed from Paphos, they came to Perga in Pamphylia: and John departing from them returned to Jerusalem." Acts 13:6-13

As they went through the isle unto Paphos preaching, we are introduced to two people that they encounter. Verse six tells us of a certain sorcerer, a false prophet, a Jew, whose name was Barjesus, or by interpretation, his name was Elymas. In verse seven we are told that he was with the deputy of the country, a man by the name of Sergius Paulus. He is described as being a prudent or wise man and that he had called Barnabas and Saul, desiring to hear the word of God.

Elymas, who is the sorcerer, withstood Barnabas and Saul, trying to turn the deputy away from the faith. In verse nine we are told, "Then Saul, (who also is called Paul,) filled with the Holy Ghost, set his eyes on him." Up until this time, Paul had been called "Saul of Tarsus", but from this moment on he is called Paul.

Paul is said to be "filled with the Holy Ghost" showing that God gave him the power and boldness to stand against this evil influence. He confronted Elymas. Criswell tells us that "the Bible is against all sorcery, witchcraft, astrological prognostications, and all the divinations that mediums and spiritists are supposed to deliver to us." Satan perverts religion and that's exactly what Elymas was trying to do is standing against these men of God. He did not want Sergius Paulus to hear the Word and be saved.

In verse nine we are told that spirit filled Paul "set his eyes on him", talking about Elymas. Paul showed holy boldness in the face of this wicked man and looked him right in the eye. In verse 10 Paul tells Elymas exactly what he is. He tells him that he is "full of all subtilty and all mischief". Remember the description of the serpent in Genesis 3:1,

"Now the serpent was more subtil than any beast of the field which the Lord God had made." Then Paul tells him that he is "the child of the devil". Elymas who was "Barjesus" which means "the son of Jesus" is told by Paul that he is no other that "the child of the devil".

He further tells him that in his deception that he is the "enemy of all righteousness". Elymas resembled his father in that he was crafty and full of malice, full of mischief. His standing against the preaching of Christ by the men God had sent the message, and shows him to be the enemy of all righteousness. Those that had come to preach Christ and salvation to Sergius Paulus were facing opposition from the devil, through Elymas, trying to keep Sergius Paulus from being saved. Remember this, when you are telling others about Jesus, the devil is not going to like it and so therefore you can always expect opposition to come.

In verse 11 Paul performs his first miracle in his ministry by bringing blindness to Elymas. The evil influence is blinded so that the light can shine forth to Sergius Paulus. God removed the obstacle that stood between him and the saving grace of God. Now instead of Elymas leading others in the wrong way, now "he went about seeking some to lead him by the hand."

Criswell says, "This powerful testimony (of Paul) is delivered only in the power of the Spirit. Were it not for the power of the Holy Spirit of God, Christianity long ago would have been swallowed up by the darkness of the world. It is in the power of the Holy Spirit that Jesus lives, moves, converts and saves."

Verse 12 tells us that when the deputy "saw what was done, believed, being astonished at the doctrine of the Lord." Before, he was having a hard time understanding, but now the scales have been removed and he can see the amazing doctrine of the Lord. Seeing the truth of God's Word and the salvation He offers through Christ, once you receive it, always causes a hunger for more.

Obstacles and oppositions come in various ways. They may not always appear in our path as another person who is being used by the devil to hinder the gospel. Sometimes it can come from within us. We don't feel like we are good enough to be doing what we are doing. Someone else could probably do it better. Many times we, and the thoughts of our minds, (that are not based on Biblical principle nor on truth) will be the biggest obstacles that we will have to deal with. If the devil can get us to thinking that what we are doing is not important or that we are not the best qualified to do the job, then he has won the battle. Don't listen to his lies! Pray, get in the Word of God, trust your calling and depend upon the Holy Spirit to strengthen you and guide you and He will give you the victory. Don't let anything or anyone stand in the way of getting the gospel message to the lost and dying people of this old world!

PERGA IN PAMPHYLIA

In Acts 13:13 tells us that Paul and his company left Paphos and sailed to Perga in Pamphylia. It was here that John Mark left this missionary company. We are not told the reason for his leaving, but none the less, he left them and returned to Jerusalem. We will hear about him again. Perga was a noted place. It was here that a temple was erected to the goddess Diana. We are not told what they did here, only that they came and they departed.

"But when they departed from Perga, they came to Antioch in Pisidia, and went into the synagogue on the sabbath day, and sat down. 15 And after the reading of the law and the prophets the

rulers of the synagogue sent unto them, saying, Ye men and brethren, if ye have any word of exhortation for the people, say on. 16 Then Paul stood up, and beckoning with his hand said, Men of Israel, and ye that fear God, give audience." Acts 13:14-16

When they came to Antioch of Pisidia, (this is a different Antioch from where they began their journey, which was Antioch in Syria) they immediately went to the synagogue for it was the sabbath day and there they sat down. After the reading of the law and prophets, the ruler of the synagogue asked Paul and Barnabas if they had any words of exhortation for the people. Paul immediately stood up and began his message of salvation.

We read Paul's message in verses 17 through 41 in the 13th chapter of Acts and as we read, the message sounds strangely familiar. It seems like we have heard it before. In it Paul recounts how God has dealt with Israel all the way to the coming of Christ. He tells them that all the promises of the Lord in the Old Testament are fulfilled in Christ. The message seems familiar because it is the message Stephen preach in the Cilician synagogue before the Sanhedrin of the Jewish nation. Saul of Tarsus was listening as he heard Stephen deliver this message. He was still meditating on this message when the Lord met him on the Damascus Road. Saul had persecuted the church and had stood by and held the garments of those who stoned Stephen to death. His message so moved the heart of Saul that he could not get away from the truth that had been presented. Now this Saul has been converted and picked up the torch to preach this message to the Jews and Gentiles in Pisidian Antioch.

Criswell tells us the heart of this message is found in Acts 13:26, "*Men and brethren, children of the stock of Abraham, and whosoever among you feareth God, to you is the word of salvation sent.*" The Greek word for "word" here is *logos*. We see it used in John 1:1 where it says, In the beginning was the Word, and the Word was with God, and the Word was God. The Word applies to God, to the Holy Scriptures, to the revelation of God's grace in the blessed Jesus. He says "to you is the word of salvation sent."

The conclusion of Paul's message is in Acts 13:38-41.

"38 Be it known unto you therefore, men and brethren, that through this man is preached unto you the forgiveness of sins: 39 And by him all that believe are justified from all things, from which ye could not be justified by the law of Moses. 40 Beware therefore, lest that come upon you, which is spoken of in the prophets; 41 Behold, ye despisers, and wonder, and perish: for I work a work in your days, a work which ye shall in no wise believe, though a man declare it unto you."

Paul's message has to do with the forgiveness of sins and our justification before God. He had preached a lengthy message about Jesus. The Jews question now must be "What is all this to us". Paul answers them with "through this man is preached unto you the forgiveness of sins." He tells them that for all that believe, they can be justified from all things." Then he warns them not to put Christ away, for he said the Lord had warned through the prophets, for I work a work in your days, a work which ye shall not believe, though a man declare it unto you." He pleads with them, do not turn Him away. Oh how people need this message of the grace of the Son of God; that God has made provision for our cleansing and for our forgiveness.

Acts 13:42-48 says, "And when the Jews were gone out of the synagogue, the Gentiles besought that these words might be preached to them the next sabbath. 43 Now when the congregation was broken up, many of the Jews and religious proselytes followed Paul and Barnabas: who, speaking to them, persuaded them to continue in the grace of God. 44 And the next sabbath day came almost the whole city together to hear the word of God. 45 But when the Jews saw the multitudes, they were filled with envy, and spake against those things which were spoken by Paul, contradicting and blaspheming. 46 Then Paul and Barnabas waxed bold, and said, It was necessary that the word of God should first have been spoken to you: but seeing ye put it from you, and judge yourselves unworthy of everlasting life, lo, we turn to the Gentiles. 47 For so hath the Lord commanded us, saying, I have set thee to be a light of the Gentiles, that thou shouldest be for salvation unto the ends of the earth. 48 And when the Gentiles heard this, they were glad, and glorified the word of the Lord: and as many as were ordained to eternal life believed."

THE WORD OF GOD PREACHED

Dr. Criswell tells us that Chapter 13 of Acts refers to the Word of the Lord seven different times. It is mentioned in verse 5: *"And when they were at Salamis, they preached the word of God ..."* It is mentioned again in verse 26: *"... to you is the word of this salvation sent."* We see God's Word referred to again in verse 42: *"... the Gentiles besought that these words might be preached to them ..."* It is mentioned in verse 44: *"And the next sabbath day came almost the whole city together to hear the word of God."* It is mentioned again in verse 46: *"... It was necessary that the word of God should first have been spoken to you..."* In verse 48 we read: *"And when the Gentiles heard this, they were glad, and glorified the word of the Lord..."* And finally in verse 49 we read: *"And the word of the Lord was published throughout all the region."* How important the Word of God is in missions. It is the act of telling the story of Jesus to those who have never heard. The mention of the Word of God is to show the means of expressing God's love to a lost and dying world through Christ and His shed blood. What a glorious thing to be called by God as instruments to be used of Him in teaching and preaching the Word of God!

Paul had stood and used the Word of God to show the Jews how God has sent Jesus to be salvation for them. Dr. Sightler in his book on Acts gives us four tremendous truths that Paul delivered. 1. He proclaims a miracle Master; 2. He delivers a miracle Message; 3. He preached a miracle Method; and then 4. He gave a miracle Measure. He told these Jews that through Jesus they could be "justified from all things, from which ye could not be justified by the law of Moses."

When the Jews were gone out of the building the Gentiles came asking Paul and Barnabas to preach these words to them on the next Sabbath. On the next Sabbath, almost the whole city came out to hear the word of God. Dr. Sightler says that the Word of God has never lost its appeal; the Word of God has never lost its attraction. This caused another opposition from the Jews, who were angered by the multitude that had come out. They then began to speak against the things Paul had preached.

There's always going to be some of the devils crowd, whether religious or worldly, that will try to stand against the man of God who will stand and faithfully proclaim Christ as Savior. The Jews contradicted their message from God, and even blasphemed. These remember, are religious folk who are fighting against the gospel message.

But Paul and Barnabas being bold through the power of the Holy Spirit, addressed these Jews. He told them that they should have had the message of Jesus and His salvation preached to them first and that is what he had done the sabbath before. But since they had rejected the message, Paul tells them that he turned to the Gentiles with the same message. He then proclaims to them his calling from the Lord that he had been set a light to the Gentiles to preach salvation to them throughout the whole world.

Dr. Sightler says, "I am a Gentile believer in the Lord Jesus Christ. We Gentile people have no religious heritage. Our forefathers built no temples, they wrote no Scriptures, they had no prophets. Our forefathers were barbarians. You know the average person in the continental United States of America, have grandparents who came over here from the continent of Europe. The peoples of Europe two thousand years ago were barbarians. They worshiped pagan gods which do not exist. . . It is no small wonder when Paul announced to them that he had been sent by the will of God, to be a light to Gentiles, "that thou shouldest be for salvation unto the ends of the earth."

I am saved today because of Paul's ministry to the Gentiles. My ancestors at some point in time heard the gospel and got saved and then taught their children about salvation through Christ. The message would have never reached me had Paul not preached to the Gentiles. We owe him a lot. God had a plan for all to be saved and He's carrying it out through Paul.

The Gentiles were glad and many of them accepted Christ as their Savior that very day. The phrase used here *"and as many as were ordained to eternal life believed,"* has been confused in its meaning by some. Let's look at some Scriptures and see if we can understand what it means. Hebrews 5:9 tells us that Christ became the author of eternal salvation. Romans 10:13 teaches us, *"For whosoever shall call upon the name of the Lord shall be saved."* In John 3:16 it says, *"For God so loved the world, that he gave his only begotten Son, that whosoever believeth in him should not perish, but have everlasting life."*

THE WORD OF GOD PREACHED – Continued

Look at what Peter said in II Peter 3: 9, "*The Lord is not slack concerning his promise, as some men count slackness; but is long-suffering to us-ward, not willing that any should perish, but that all should come to repentance.*" Look at what Paul says in 1Timothy 2:3, 4, "*For this is good and acceptable in the sight of God our Saviour; Who will have all men to be saved, and - to come unto the knowledge of the truth.*"

For some to say that these men were ordained to salvation meaning that God had decided that in eternity past they would be saved, leaves us with the assumption then that those who didn't get saved, were ordained to be lost for eternity. That simply does not align with the Word of God. How can a God who wants all men to be saved only pick and choose a few along the way? How could a loving God, after all that He has done to make a plan of salvation for man, exclude some from eternal life? According to the Scriptures this will never happen. The Scriptural way is if you can believe!

Then we ask the question, "Does God choose men?" The answer is yes. Criswell tells us that it is a fact in the Holy Scriptures. He chose Abraham out of idolatry. He chose Moses and sent him down into the land of Egypt. He chose Aaron, and He chose the Levites for the ministries in the tabernacle. He chose David and anointed him above his brethren. He chose the twelve apostles. He intervened in the life of the archpersecutor, Saul of Tarsus. God chose him and made him the apostle Paul. Yes God chooses!

Criswell also tells us that man has a choice. We too can choose what we are going to do. God made us free. We are human agents able to choose for ourselves. We are free, but we are morally responsible. We can choose for ourselves.

Moses stood in the midst of the camp as the Israelites danced naked around the golden calf and called, saying, *"Who is on the Lord's side? Let him some unto me."* Exodus 32:26.

The Captain of the host of Israel, Joshua, closes his book with an address in which he concludes, *"Choose you this day whom ye will serve . . . but as for me and my house, we will serve the Lord."* Joshua 24:15. In 1 Kings 18:21, Elijah is on top of Mt. Carmel saying to the people of Israel, *"If the Lord be God, follow him, but if Baal, then follow him"*. The power of choice is given to us.

The invitations of the Scripture show us this truth. Jesus said, *"Come unto me, all ye that labour and are heavy laden, and I will give you rest"* Matthew 11:28. In the last invitation in the book of Revelation it says, *"And the Spirit and the bride say, Come. And let him that heareth say, Come. And let him that is athirst come. And whosoever will, let him take the water of life freely"* Revelation 22:17.

These Gentiles who were saved put their faith in the finished work of Christ on the cross. The Jews who had heard earlier, failed to accept the salvation offered them. This is the free will of man. When we are presented with the Gospel message, we have the choice to either accept Him or reject Him! These Gentiles chose to accept. Others who heard that day chose to reject. That does not mean that they cannot be saved. It does mean that they might be presented with the Gospel message at another time and chose to accept it then or they might never be saved, but it is their choice. God has already chosen all to be saved through the blood of Jesus if they will only believe!

I think the important thing here is that men were saved!

Many places that Paul and Barnabas visited in their missionary journey had people saved. Keep in mind that all the things that Paul and his team did as they travelled from place to place are not talked about in the book of Acts. Many souls were saved and churches established along the way, because God was guiding them, the Spirit was filling them and they were willing to obey!

Acts 13:49-52 says, "And the word of the Lord was published throughout all the region. 50 But the Jews stirred up the devout and honourable women, and the chief men of the city, and raised persecution against Paul and Barnabas, and expelled them out of their coasts. 51 But they shook off the dust of their feet against them, and came unto Iconium. 52 And the disciples were filled with joy, and with the Holy Ghost."

Here's the good news, not only were there Gentiles saved here through the preaching of the Word, but "the word of the Lord was published throughout all the region." There's no telling what effect this message had on the region around Antioch and how many people were saved as a result of this preaching.

In verse 50 the devils stirs up the Jews in Antioch of Pisidia. Here is more opposition to the Word of God being preached. The devil hates it. This time the opposition becomes so strong that Paul and Barnabas are expelled from Antioch and driven out of their coasts.

So the missionary endeavor that Paul and Barnabas had started in the beginning of this chapter ends in tumult, in a persecution, in an expelling from the city and from the whole country.

As they walked out of the city verse 51 tells us that they "shook the dust off their feet (as a testimony) against them *and came to Iconium"*. The disciples left with rejoicing, letting others know that they were happy with their relationship with God and with the word of God which had brought salvation to them and they were filled with the Spirit of God that they might continue to be effective in their service for Him.

AT ICONIUM

As we study Chapter 14 it is important that we look at verse 27 as a background for the whole chapter.

Acts. 14:27 says "And when they were come, and had gathered the church together, they rehearsed all that God had done with them, and how he had opened the door of faith unto the Gentiles."

Acts 14:1 says, "And it came to pass in Iconium, that they went both together into the synagogue of the Jews, and so spake, that a great multitude both of the Jews and also of the Greeks believed.

Paul and Barnabas had found what works in reaching people for Christ. They preached the Word of God. Paul and Barnabas speak and multitudes of Jews and Greeks and Gentiles, believed and were converted.

Acts 14:2, "But the unbelieving Jews stirred up the Gentiles, and made their minds evil affected against the brethren."

Just as the unbelieving Jews had done in Antioch of Pisidia, they are doing it again here in Iconium. Dr. Sightler points out that the fact is that everywhere Paul goes on his missionary journeys for some 35 years, he is going to run into opposition from unbelieving Jews; and they are going to give him opposition everywhere and on every hand. Dr. Sightler reminds us of a lesson he has learned that the preaching of the Gospel is not popular. . . The grace of God has never been popular. The Word of God has never been popular with the masses. He says, "It is popular with me and you who know the Lord and who love the Lord, but the unbelieving Jews will stir up people against the preaching of the Word of God. Verse 2 says, *"and made their minds evil affected against the brethren."* They brainwashed the people to believe that Barnabas and Paul were reprobates and renegades. Thus, they caused them not to trust them or their preaching.

Acts 14:3-4, "Long time therefore abode they speaking boldly in the Lord, which gave testimony unto the word of his grace, and granted signs and wonders to be done by their hands. 4 But the multitude of the city was divided: and part held with the Jews, and part with the apostles."

In spite of the opposition they faced, they continued their work there a long time. They worked faithfully and diligently with the people though there were those there who hated what they were doing and would never stop trying to stop them, to shut them up and to run them off. They were afraid to do the work God had sent them to do. They spoke boldly in the Lord.

Matthew Henry reminds us that the gospel is a word of grace, the assurance of God's good will to us and the means of his good work in us. It is the word of Christ's grace, for it is in him alone that we find favor with God.

They had come to Iconium to preach the gospel, but how did that end?

Acts 14:5 says "And when there was an assault made both of the Gentiles, and also of the Jews with their rulers, to use them despitefully, and to stone them. "

The people, especially the religious crowd, rejected the

teachings of Paul and Barnabas, but despite the opposition, the message was still preached and many were saved as a result.

According to verse 3, the Lord was pleased with the faithful work of His servants, Paul and Barnabas, there in Iconium. Dr. Sightler said that the signs and wonders done among them was a special smile of God's approval before the unbelieving Jews upon the ministry of Paul and Barnabas.

He further states that "to the Apostles, God indeed gave signs and miracles to the degree that they actually, literally resurrected dead people. Nobody in the world can do such a thing in our day. There is not one single man in all the earth; and there has not been since the apostles died, who can resurrect the dead. And there will be nobody in the world who can do so on tomorrow. This was a sign granted by God only to the apostles; and here is a demonstration of something of this miracle signs and miracle wonders being done by their hands as they preached the Word of God here. But in spite of the signs, there was still a division among the people. Not everyone believed the message, nor the signs and wonders from God. "The multitude of the city was divided." No matter how hard we try in our day to get the gospel message to every soul, every one that hears the message is not going to accept it. Many will let the message go unheeded. Some will think that it is for someone else and not for them. They will turn the message of salvation away and walk on in their sin away from God. Hence, it is not our calling to make them believe, but rather to make sure they get the message. What they do with it is up to them, but we must deliver the message!

LYSTRA AND DERBE

Acts 14:6 – 7 tells us "They were ware of it, and fled unto Lystra and Derbe, cities of Lycaonia, and unto the region that lieth around about: 7 And there they preached the gospel."

Persecution and rejection and even the possibility of being killed did not stop them from doing what God had called them to do. They fled for their lives from Iconium when they saw that their lives were in danger, but they continued what they were doing when they came into Lystra and Derbe, for they preached the gospel. They continued to preach the word of God and continued to proclaim the word of God in all of its power and in all of its purity.

We see some great things happened when they came to Iconium, "They preached the gospel with great boldness", and great grace was upon the people. We see that the first missionary journey was characterized by the fact that they faithfully preached the word of God. So powerful was the word that verse 48 said, *"And when the Gentiles heard this, they were glad, and glorified the word of God".* They did not glorify Paul or Barnabas, but they "glorified the word of God." As a result many of them were saved!

Acts 14: 8 - 10 says, "And there sat a certain man at Lystra, impotent in his feet, being a cripple from his mother's womb, who never had walked: 9 The same heard Paul speak: who stedfastly beholding him, and perceiving that he had faith to be healed, 10 Said with a loud voice, Stand upright on thy feet. And he leaped and walked."

Notices that the man is not mentioned by name, it only says, "a certain man". It is not for show or for this man's glory, but for the glory of God. The problem that He is facing is that he is impotent in his feet. He was a cripple man who had been this way from his mother's womb. He had never walked in his whole lifetime. He had never taken a step.

Dr. Sightler says that if anything, the emphasis of the condition of the man shows him that all men out of Christ are without God and without hope . . . All men are twice dead and plucked up by the roots until they come to know the Savior, the Lord Jesus Christ. So the man that Paul is about to heal is a hopeless, helpless cripple from his mother's womb.

As Paul preaches, he notices this man, "beholding him" and perceives that he has faith to be healed. So Paul singles him out and with a loud voice says to him, "Stand upright on thy feet". This was something that the man had never done and probably no one there that day thought that he ever could. But when Paul spoke to him in a loud voice, immediately, the man not only stood up, but leaped up and walked, because God had healed him by His great power.

Matthew Henry said that men are "lame from their birth, till the grace of God puts strength into them, for it was when "we were yet without strength that Christ died for the ungodly, Romans 5:6." Thank God for His healing touch on fallen man!

Acts 14:11-13 says, "And when the people saw what Paul had done, they lifted up their voices, saying in the speech of Lycaonia, The gods are come down to us in the likeness of men. 12 And they called Barnabas, Jupiter; and Paul, Mercurius, because he was the chief speaker. 13 Then the priest of Jupiter, which was before their city, brought oxen and garlands unto the gates, and would have done sacrifice with the people."

It is clear from these verses that these people worshipped

many gods. Notices they said in verse 11, "the gods" and not one god. The gods have come down to us, they said. We understand that they are pagan people and they are wanting to make two human people, Paul and Barnabas, gods, because they had healed this cripple man. We see that they were actually planning an animal sacrifice at the gate of Lystra.

The people gave these Apostles new names, supposing that they had been sent down to them from some higher power of their pagan theology. They named Barnabas, Jupiter who was the prince of their gods. Paul they named, Mercury, who was the messenger of the gods that was sent to run errands, because he was the chief speaker.

When they prepared to do sacrifice to them they were at the temple of Jupiter which was located at the gate of the city, probably because they looked at him to be a protector or guardian. How easily vain minds are carried away with a popular outcry. All the people are ready to join in the sacrifice with them.

This seems to be a strange thing indeed for people to do, but people in our day, two thousand years later, still worship all kinds of strange gods. Many worship and bow down to money. Some bow down to pleasures. Others bow down to lusts. Some pagans in the world worship the stars and moon and planets and even animals. We see in the thing that happened here in Lystra that when the gospel is preached, light floods the darkness of the false religions of the world.

PAUL AND BARNABAS'S REACTION

Acts 4:14-15 says, "Which when the apostles, Barnabas and Paul, heard of, they rent their clothes, and ran in among the

*people, crying out, 15 And saying, Sirs, why do ye these things?
We also are men of like passions with you, and preach unto you
that ye should turn from these vanities unto the living God, which
made heaven, and earth, and the sea, and all things that are
therein:"*

When Paul and Barnabas heard what they were planning
to do they rent their clothes and ran in among the people,
crying out. Matthew Henry gives several reasons of how
they prevented the sacrifice. First they ran among the people
as soon as they heard what they were planning to do. Then
they reasoned with them saying "Sirs, why do you these
things." They told them that (1) their nature will no admit it,
"we are also men of like passions with you." (2) Our
doctrine is directly against it. We're preaching that you turn
away for these vanities.

Paul tells them the message that all the world needs to
know, that there is only one God. He boldly proclaims that
God made all things. One God and one mediator between
God and man, the man Christ Jesus. All men were made in
the creative power of Almighty God. Paul certifies this faith
in verse 15.

*Acts 14:16-18 then says, "Who in times past suffered all
nations to walk in their own ways. 17 Nevertheless he left not
himself without witness, in that he did good, and gave us rain from
heaven, and fruitful seasons, filling our hearts with food and
gladness. 18 And with these sayings scarce restrained they the
people, that they had not done sacrifice unto them."*

The words given *"suffered all nations to walk in their own
ways"* are telling us that as a judgment upon all nations, God
suffered them (or permitted them) to walk in their own
ways, gave them up to their own hearts' lusts; but now the
time is come when this will all change. They will no longer

THE MISSIONARY JOURNEYS OF PAUL

be excused in their vanities, but now they must turn from them. In presenting what God has done and will do, the people wanting to sacrifice to them are restrained. By presenting them with the Word of God, the darkness of their hearts saw the light and they ceased from the wicked thing they were about to do.

JEWS FROM ANTIOCH

Acts 4:19-20 says, "And there came thither Jews from Antioch and Iconium, who persuaded the people, and having stoned Paul, drew him out of the city, supposing he had been dead.
20 Howbeit, as the disciples stood round about him, he rose up, and came into the city: and the next day he departed with Barnabas to Derbe."

These are the Jews from Antioch of Pisidia that we read about in Chapter 13. They had tormented Paul and Barnabas and when they left that city, the Apostles shook the dust off of their feet as a testimony against them. Even though Paul and Barnabas had travelled to Iconium, these Jews had followed them. They had moved to Lystra and here Paul had healed a crippled man. The Jews, we now see, has followed them here. Everywhere Paul and Barnabas went they faced opposition. Paul is stoned and left for dead as they move him outside the city. But Paul revives and gets up and goes back into the city. God's faithful servants may be as 2 Cor. 4:9 says, *"cast down, but not destroyed."* Matthew Henry says that all the stones they threw could not beat him off from his work. Once revived he went back into the city, but then they knowing their work here for now was finished, they moved on to Derbe the next day.

PAUL AND BARNABAS'S RETURN TRIP

Acts 4:21-22 says, "And when they had preached the gospel to

*that city, and had taught many, they returned again to Lystra, and
to Iconium, and Antioch, 22 Confirming the souls of the disciples,
and exhorting them to continue in the faith, and that we must
through much tribulation enter into the kingdom of God."*

Upon arriving at Derbe, they immediately took up the
work the Holy Spirit had sent them to do. They preached the
gospel to the city and they taught those in the city. While
nothing else is mentioned here that happened in Derbe, it
should be noted that Timothy was from Derbe and no doubt
was with Paul and Barnabas here. Paul tells him in his letter
to young Timothy, *"But thou hast fully known my doctrine,
manner of life, purpose , faith, longsuffering, charity, patience,
Persecutions, afflictions, which came to me at Antioch, at Iconium,
at Lystra; what persecutions I endured: but out of them all the
Lord delivered me."*

At this point in the ministry they return to the places they
have already preached. They are "confirming the souls" of
the disciples. No doubt some of the disciples that had seen
the persecution of Paul and Barnabas were thinking if it was
worth it at all. Paul confirms them or preaches to them about
the blessed assurance that they have in Jesus. He preaches
and teaches to them messages and lesson on how they can
know that they are truly saved. It would have been a
common thought among the people to have just abandoned
the faith, because of the persecution they had seen, but Paul
comes back to them and reminds them that everything is all
right in the Father's House. He encourages them to press on.
He persuades them to go on in the faith of God. Don't give
up. Don't ever quit! Dr. Sightler says that he reminds them
that tribulation is a common experience which will befall
those who enter into the kingdom of God and who are truly
born of God's Spirit. So Paul tells them to lift up their heads
and endure the tribulation heaped upon them to the glory
and to the honor of God. What an example of faithfulness

this is to you and me!

Acts 14:23 says, *"And when they had ordained them elders in every church, and had prayed with fasting, they commended them to the Lord, on whom they believed."*

This is an important verse for we find here the mention of the local church. Notice he said, "every church". In every church they ordained elders. Probably done by calling all the believers together and voting on a man of God to lead the church. This verse teaches us according to Dr. Sightler that "every local church is an independent, autonomous, local congregation, self-governing, and self-determining in its own authority. . . All the churches mentioned in the New Testament are local church congregations. . . The plan of God is that every local congregation ordain its own elders, send out its own missionaries, as in the case of chapter 13 with the church at Antioch, and to mind its own business, ordain its own deacons, and carry on its own work."

The churches chose these elders after having prayed and fasted about the matter. Once sure of the will of God, they commended them to the Lord, or approved them for the office they had been chosen.

Acts 14:24-25 says, *"And after they had passed throughout Pisidia, they came to Pamphylia. 25 And when they had preached the word in Perga, they went down into Attalia:"*

They are again returning to the places that they have preached at and have had people saved in. Their purpose is to check up on them and make sure they are strong in the faith and continuing to follow the Lord. They were laying a foundation that could be built on later. Notice that they preached the word in Perga. We don't know the results of the preaching, but God was using His servants to preach the gospel of Christ.

Acts 14: 26 says, "And thence sailed to Antioch, from whence they had been recommended to the grace of God for the work which they fulfilled."

Back to the place they began this ministry. The first missionary journey began in Chapter 13 as the church sends out Barnabas and Paul to do the work which they were called to do and we're told they did the work faithfully (they fulfilled the work). Now we see it ends at the end of Chapter 14 after Paul and Barnabas had literally done exactly that which they were sent out to do by the Holy Spirit.

Acts 14:27 say, "And when they were come, and had gathered the church together, they rehearsed all that God had done with them, and how he had opened the door of faith unto the Gentiles."

When Paul and Barnabas arrived back at the place where they had begun their missionary journey, they called the church together to give a report of what they had done. I believe it to be an important thing that the missionary report to the church about what is going on in their particular field of service. What a thrill it must have been for the Christians that had sent these missionaries out to now sit and hear them tell how God had opened doors and multitudes were saved. There's nothing like sending a missionary out from your church, support his labors and pray for him and his family on a daily basis and then have them return and report about what God had done in people's lives because of their labors.

So the church at Antioch gathered together for a mission conference so that Paul and Barnabas could "rehearse" what God had done as they preached. They did not stand and tell of the hardships of the journey; of the near death experiences; of the persecution they faced along the way. But they told how God had worked in salvation and how the churches were established and how many of those who were saved are now tell others about the salvation they received through the Lord Jesus Christ.

Acts. 14:28 says, "And there they abode long time with the disciples."

This first missionary journey ends with rejoicing in the church because of all the things that God had done through these two men, Paul and Barnabas, which they had sent out to preach the gospel. Matthew Henry suggests that they "abode long time with the disciples," longer than perhaps at first they intended, not because they feared their enemies, but because they loved their friends, and were loath to part from them.

The Second Missionary Journey

NEED FOR COUNCIL CONCERNING CIRCUMCISION

INTRO: BETWEEN THE FIRST TWO JOURNEYS

Remember that Acts 14 had ended with these two verses. Acts 14:27, 28, "*And when they were come, and had gathered the church together, they rehearsed all that God had done with them, and how he had opened the door of faith unto the Gentiles. 28 And there they abode long time with the disciples.*"

This tells us that there was a period of time between the first missionary journey and the second missionary journey. We want to look at some of the things the Scripture tells us that happened during this time.

No doubt they were rejoicing because of the success of the first missionary journey. I believe also that there was a lot that Paul and Barnabas could teach the church here about missions.

Acts 15:1 says, "*And certain men which came down from Judaea taught the brethren, and said, Except ye be circumcised after the manner of Moses, ye cannot be saved.*"

This chapter records the first general council of the newly instituted church in Jerusalem. We are told they are called together because of a dispute among some of the leaders of the church of Jerusalem concerning circumcision being essential for a Gentile to be saved. Dr. Sightler says that we find in the church in Galatia, there were some Jewish believers who came to the Galatian believers and insisted they be circumcised after the custom of the Law of Moses in order to be a Gentile believer in the Lord Jesus Christ. Paul disputed with them and stated that their salvation was based entirely upon the matter of faith, a personal faith in the Lord Jesus without the deeds of the law and without the rite of Jewish circumcision. He told them that the Gentiles were not required to be circumcised in order to be a disciple of the Lord Jesus.

Paul makes mention of this in his letter to the Galatians in chapters 1 and 2. These men that had come down said, "Except ye be circumcised after the manner of Moses, ye cannot be saved." What they said is that, you say you are a Christian, but without circumcision, we do not accept you as a follower of Christ. This was a disturbing statement and one that must be cleared up because of the Gentiles that had accepted Christ and many other Gentiles that would be saved.

Dr. Criswell says, "What they are saying is: A man cannot be saved by trusting Jesus alone. In order to be saved, one must trust Jesus, and he must do something else."

Paul had written to the Galatians in chapter 5:2, 4, 6 and said, "Behold, I Paul say unto you, that if ye be circumcised, Christ shall profit you nothing. 4 Christ is become of no effect unto you, whosoever of you are justified by the law; ye are fallen from grace. 6 For in Jesus Christ neither circumcision availeth any thing, nor uncircumcision; but faith which worketh by love. "

Acts 15:2 says, *"When therefore Paul and Barnabas had no small dissension and disputation with them, they determined that Paul and Barnabas, and certain other of them, should go up to Jerusalem unto the apostles and elders about this question."*

The "they" mentioned in verse 2 is referring to the church at Antioch. They determined that they would go to Jerusalem and get this matter settled once and for all. This was important to the Gentiles saved in Antioch and Galatia and Jerusalem and all of Paul's newly instituted congregations. So the church sends Paul and Barnabas along with several others, up to Jerusalem to debate the question and to get it settled finally and completely.

Acts 15:3, 4 says, *"And being brought on their way by the church, they passed through Phenice and Samaria, declaring the conversion of the Gentiles: and they caused great joy unto all the brethren. And when they were come to Jerusalem, they were received of the church, and of the apostles and elders, and they declared all things that God had done with them."*

It says in verse 3 that they were brought on their way by the church, which means that they were taken care of by the church. All their expenses were taken care of by the church. I'm sure there were a lot of financial expense in their journey as well as many spiritual needs they would face. The church knew that it was important to the life of the church that this problem be taken care of. If they were to continue to prosper, this issue concerning salvation had to be settled. We should be mindful of the weight of the burden that the missionary carries today. We should be able to help them both financially and spiritually in their labors.

As they passed through Phenice and Samaria they preached the conversion of the Gentiles which caused great joy to all the brethren. When they came into Jerusalem they were received, first of all by the church and then by the apostles and elders who were members of the church. Here they reported to the church all that the Lord had done with them. Their testimony alone of the many Gentiles that had been saved on the first missionary journey should have been sufficient to settle the matter they had come to debate.

Acts 15:5-6 says, *"But there rose up certain of the sect of the Pharisees which believed, saying, That it was needful to circumcise them, and to command them to keep the law of Moses. 6 And the apostles and elders came together for to consider of this matter."*

Notice the problem was from a sect of the Pharisees that were saying circumcision was necessary for a person to be saved. This was a group of Pharisees it is said "which believed." Apparently they believed the wrong thing in order to be saved.

Jesus and the early Church had a number of conflicts with the Pharisees. Read Matthew 23 to understand better what Jesus thought of their teaching. Jesus called them "blind guides" in verse 16. He called them fools in verse 17. In verse 27, He says they are like whited sepulchers, full of dead men's bones, and all uncleanness. He calls them serpents in verse 33 and also refers to them as a generation of vipers.

To be able to see some of the wrong teachings of the Pharisees consider the Pharisee's meticulous approach to Sabbath-keeping, they really stand out as an interesting case study in how religion can be done wrong. Here is a list of a few of their Sabbath traditions:

The Pharisees didn't permit people to carry mats about on the Sabbath. John chapter 5 tells us about how Jesus permitted a man He had just healed to carry his mat. The Pharisees focused more on the fact that one of their traditions were broken than that a person was miraculously healed!

They also didn't permit people to carry clothing with them on the Sabbath, unless they were wearing it. If a person's house caught fire on the Sabbath, a person wouldn't have been allowed to save an article of clothing by carrying it out. However, they were permitted to put on as much clothing as they could and leave their house with what they were wearing!

They also didn't permit people to carry metal around with them on the Sabbath. The nails that were in a person's shoes were included in the prohibition, so many people had special Sabbath footwear!

They considered spitting on the ground a no-no on the Sabbath. The reasoning was that plowing was a kind of work, and they defined "plowing" as any act that disturbed the ground, even slightly. And, as they saw it, the slight disturbance caused by spitting was enough to be considered work!

The Pharisees only permitted people to travel a certain distance from their home on the Sabbath. They also defined their home as where their doorpost was located, so some of them removed their doorpost from its place and took it with them, and in so doing, they were permitted to travel as far as they wished on the Sabbath. Not only did they develop their own traditions, they developed their own work-arounds! *(https://truthsower.wordpress.com/2019/11/02/the-pharisees-a-case-study-in-religion-gone-wrong/)*

THE COUNCILS DECISION

Verse 6 tells us that the apostles and elders came together to consider the matter. They were trying to nail down once and for all just how men were to be saved. Were the Gentiles to be saved the same way the Jews were. Was it supposed to be by faith or were they to add the works of the law to salvation? This was the question they were to discuss and what a powerful question it was.

Matthew Henry says that they did not come to give their separate judgments on the subject, but came together to . . .

hear one another's sense in this matter. He says, for in the multitude of counsellors there is safety.

Acts 15:7 – 11 says, *"And when there had been much disputing, Peter rose up, and said unto them, Men and brethren, ye know how that a good while ago God made choice among us, that the Gentiles by my mouth should hear the word of the gospel, and believe. 8 And God, which knoweth the hearts, bare them witness, giving them the Holy Ghost, even as he did unto us; 9 And put no difference between us and them, purifying their hearts by faith. 10 Now therefore why tempt ye God, to put a yoke upon the neck of the disciples, which neither our fathers nor we were able to bear? 11 But we believe that through the grace of the Lord Jesus Christ we shall be saved, even as they."*

When Peter speaks he is giving testimony of what took place in the house of Cornelius. It was here that God allowed Peter to preach the gospel to the Gentile household of Cornelius and as the Holy Spirit fell on the congregation and they repented and received Christ. Peter knew that what he did there was of God. He was assured that nothing else was needed for these Gentiles to be saved other that what they had received. Peter saw no reason for them to yoke the Gentiles with something that he says, "neither our fathers nor we were able to bear." Peter declared that salvation comes to the Jew and the Gentile through the grace of the Lord Jesus Christ.

Then as the counsel is quietly considering this testimony, Paul and Barnabas stand up to speak. Acts 15:12 says *"Then all the multitude kept silence, and gave audience to Barnabas and Paul, declaring what miracles and wonders God had wrought among the Gentiles by them."* They begin to again rehearse before those present the miracles and wonders that God had done to the Gentiles by their preaching to them. Testimony after testimony of those Gentiles that had been gloriously saved by Paul and Barnabas simply preaching Christ to them. There was no doubt in Paul and Barnabas's mind that God's way of salvation was "by grace through faith in Jesus Christ". Everything that was needed to be done for a person, Jew or Gentile, to be saved was done by Christ on the cross. All they needed to do was believe in the finished work of Christ, repent of their sins and accept His grace that had been extended to them.

James now, as moderator of this council, decides there has been enough testimony and steps forth to speak. Acts 15:13-21 says, "*And after they had held their peace, James answered, saying, Men and brethren, hearken unto me: 14 Simeon hath declared how God at the first did visit the Gentiles, to take out of them a people for his name. 15 And to this agree the words of the prophets; as it is written, 16 After this I will return, and will build again the tabernacle of David, which is fallen down; and I will build again the ruins thereof, and I will set it up: 17 That the residue of men might seek after the Lord, and all the Gentiles, upon whom my name is called, saith the Lord, who doeth all these things. 18 Known unto God are all his works from the beginning of the world. 19 Wherefore my sentence is, that we trouble not them, which from among the Gentiles are turned to God: 20 But that we write unto them, that they abstain from pollutions of idols, and from fornication, and from things strangled, and from blood. 21 For Moses of old time hath in every city them that preach him, being read in the synagogues every sabbath day.*"

He reminds them further of the testimony of Simeon who said that God would visit the Gentiles and take out of them a people for His name. Then he refers to the account of the prophets who declared the salvation of the Gentiles. And then James declares that the will and plan of God has been written and known from the beginning of the world. Upon these testimonies James then declares his sentence in the matter before them. He said that the Gentiles were not to be troubled with the thought of having to be circumcised to be saved. That faith in the grace of God was enough. He did declare also that the Gentiles were to be reminded to abstain from pollutions of idols and from fornication and from things strangled and from blood. That is to say, they were to keep themselves pure from the defilements of this old world.

In Acts 15:22-30 it is said, "*Then pleased it the apostles and elders, with the whole church, to send chosen men of their own company to Antioch with Paul and Barnabas; namely, Judas surnamed Barsabas, and Silas, chief men among the brethren: 23 And they wrote letters by them after this manner; The apostles and elders and brethren send greeting unto the brethren which are of the Gentiles in Antioch and Syria and Cilicia: 24 Forasmuch as we have heard, that certain which went out from us have troubled you with words, subverting your souls, saying, Ye must be circumcised, and keep the law: to whom we gave no such commandment: 25 It seemed good unto us, being assembled with one accord, to send chosen men unto you with our beloved Barnabas and Paul, 26Men that have hazarded their lives for the name of our Lord Jesus Christ. 27 We have sent therefore Judas and Silas, who shall also tell you the same things by mouth. 28 For it seemed good to the Holy Ghost, and to us, to lay upon you no greater burden than these necessary things; 29 That ye abstain from meats offered to idols, and from blood, and from things strangled, and from fornication: from which if ye keep yourselves, ye shall do well. Fare ye well. 30 So when they were dismissed, they came to Antioch: and when they had gathered the multitude together, they delivered the epistle:*"

The apostles and elders and the whole church were pleased to send Judas surnamed Barsabas and Silas to Antioch with Paul and Barnabas with letters declaring to the Gentiles the decision made by the council at Jerusalem. They wanted the Gentiles to know that the teaching that certain had been teaching concerning the need for circumcision to be saved, was not authorized by them. These two men along with the letters from the council were sent with Paul and Barnabas to verify that this indeed was the final word from the council on this matter.

They had no doubt great respect for Paul and Barnabas saying that they were men "that have hazarded their lives for the name of our Lord Jesus Christ. Verse 30 tells us that when they came to Antioch and had gathered the multitude together they delivered this letter from the council.

Acts 15:31 - 34 says, "*Which when they had read, they rejoiced for the consolation. 32 And Judas and Silas, being prophets also themselves, exhorted the brethren with many words, and confirmed them. 33 And after they had tarried there a space, they were let go in peace from the brethren unto the apostles. 34 Notwithstanding it pleased Silas to abide there still.*"

Rejoicing and confirmation is made among the Church and then these men, Judas and Silas, were released from their charge and were allowed to go back to Jerusalem. But Silas decides to stay in Antioch.

BEGINNING THE SECOND MISSIONARY JOURNEY

Acts 15: 35 – 40 says, "*Paul also and Barnabas continued in Antioch, teaching and preaching the word of the Lord, with many others also. 36 And some days after Paul said unto Barnabas, Let us go again and visit our brethren in every city where we have preached the word of the Lord, and see how they do. 37 And Barnabas determined to take with them John, whose surname was Mark. 38 But Paul thought not good to take him with them, who departed from them from Pamphylia, and went not with them to the work. 39 And the contention was so sharp between them, that they departed asunder one from the other: and so Barnabas took Mark, and sailed unto Cyprus; 40 And Paul chose Silas, and departed, being recommended by the brethren unto the grace of God."*

We are told that Paul and Barnabas continued to teach and preach the word of the Lord in Antioch along with many others. And then came the day when Paul told Barnabas that it was time for them to visit the brethren in the cities where they had already preached the word in their first missionary journey. The purpose being to check on how these believers were doing.

CONTENTION BETWEEN PAUL AND BARNABAS

Barnabas was determined that John Mark was going to go on this journey with them, but Paul didn't think that was a good idea. Paul was remembering that John Mark had left them in their first missionary journey and was not sure that he would be able or beneficial to them on this journey. The contention was so strong that these two great men had to part their ways. Barnabas took John Mark and sailed to Cyprus, his home country, while Paul took Silas and went through Syria and Cilicia, his home country, confirming the churches. The churches approval was apparently on Paul and Silas and they recommended them unto the grace of God.

Lest we think bad of John Mark, who was the writer of the Gospel of Mark, Paul just didn't think that he was as fervent in the ministry as he should be. Barnabas, on the other-hand, is known as the son of consolation and thought it to be a good idea to give Mark a second chance.

One lesson from verse 39 that Dr. Sightler points out is "that when contentions come, or difference of opinions might flair up, there is no indication in such, no reason why a man should break fellowship, not at all. We will agree and we shall disagree; but we will resolve and purpose by the

45

grace of God to love one another in spite of disagreements. . . I am inclined to believe it to be God's will for Paul to revisit these churches. But it was also God's will for Barnabas to go to his own country, Cyprus, with Mark and do a mission work there."

Later Paul had a better opinion of Mark for he writes to Timothy in 2 Timothy 4:11, "Take Mark and bring him with thee, for he is profitable to me for the ministry." And in Colossians 4:10 he mentions ". . .Marcus, sister's son to Barnabas, (touching whom ye received commandments: if he come unto you, receive him;)"

AT DERBE AND LYSTRA – INTRODUCTION TO TIMOTHY

In Acts 16:1 – 5 we are told, "*Then came he to Derbe and Lystra: and, behold, a certain disciple was there, named Timotheus, the son of a certain woman, which was a Jewess, and believed; but his father was a Greek: 2 Which was well reported of by the brethren that were at Lystra and Iconium. 3 Him would Paul have to go forth with him; and took and circumcised him because of the Jews which were in those quarters: for they knew all that his father was a Greek. 4 And as they went through the cities, they delivered them the decrees for to keep, that were ordained of the apostles and elders which were at Jerusalem. 5 And so were the churches established in the faith, and increased in number daily.*"

One of the first places mentioned that Paul and Silas came to was Derbe and Lystra. Paul and Barnabas had preached in these places before on their first missionary journey and had left many believers there. We are introduced here to a disciple by the name of Timotheus. He is the son of a Jewess woman who believed and a Greek father. We are told that he was well reported of by the brethren here. We know Timothy from the two letters that Paul would later write to him, 1 & 2 Timothy. Here Paul chooses Timothy to go with him and Silas. Paul had Timothy circumcised because of the Jews there that all knew his father was a Greek. This is a different situation than what was dealt with at the council in Jerusalem in chapter 15. Here is a man that is a believer, but he is mixture of Jew and Gentile blood. It seems that not as a means of compromise, but rather for his testimonies sake, Paul decided it best that Timothy be circumcised.

As they were revisiting the churches they had started in the first missionary journey, they delivered to them the letters that had come from the Jerusalem council. These churches were said to be established in the faith, meaning that they were solid in their standing for Christ. Also they were growing churches for verse 5 tells us they were increasing in number daily.

FROM PHRYGIA TO PHILIPPI

**PHRYGIA, GALATIA, FORBIDDEN TO PREACH IN ASIA
MYSIA, FORBIDDEN TO GO TO BITHYNIA
FROM MYSIA TO TROAS WHERE PAUL HAS A VISION
THEY LEFT TROAS AND WENT TO SAMOTHRACIA
THEN THE NEXT DAY TO NEAPOLIS THEN TO PHILIPPI**

Acts 16:6 - 12 says *"Now when they had gone throughout Phrygia and the region of Galatia, and were forbidden of the Holy Ghost to preach the word in Asia, 7 After they were come to Mysia, they assayed to go into Bithynia: but the Spirit suffered them not. 8 And they passing by Mysia came down to Troas. 9 And a vision appeared to Paul in the night; There stood a man of Macedonia, and prayed him, saying, Come over into Macedonia, and help us. 10 And after he had seen the vision, immediately we endeavored to go into Macedonia, assuredly gathering that the Lord had called us for to preach the gospel unto them. 11 Therefore loosing from Troas, we came with a straight course to Samothracia, and the next day to Neapolis; 12 And from thence to Philippi, which is the chief city of that part of Macedonia, and a colony: and we were in that city abiding certain days."*

This is a particularly special portion of Scripture to me, for it was this passage of the Word of God that the Lord used in getting me involved in missions many years ago. This is known as "The Macedonian call". Several things to notice here before we get to that though. First of all, we see that they had gone throughout Phrygia and the region of Galatia, but then the verse tells us they were "forbidden of the Holy Ghost" to preach the word in Asia". We see the leading of the Holy Spirit in their ministry. They were going into Asia to preach the Gospel message, but the Holy Spirit said no. They then when to Mysia and planned to go into Bithynia, but again the Spirit would not let them.

If you have never been led by the Spirit in this way, you are missing a real blessing. I believe they prayed about where the Lord wanted them to go next and that day by day as they preached the Word, the Spirit of God was leading them to the place He wanted them to be. That's the way many of our missionaries on the field around the world today found where God wanted them to be. First of all, you need to be preaching the Word where you are and then begin praying where else the Lord might let you preach! Don't ever expect to find the will of God for your life by sitting and doing nothing. If you won't tell people here about the Lord Jesus Christ, don't expect Him to send you to the other side of the world to minister. If you're not doing it here, you won't do it there!

Dr. Sightler tells us why they were not allowed to go to these places that the Holy Spirit forbid them to go. He said, "the reason is not because God did not desire the word be preached, but rather, the Lord had a better alternative, including the Macedonian call which would call Paul and

Silas away from Israel, even up into the continent of Europe to tell the story to barbaric people who lived on the continent of Europe two thousand years ago." Many times in our lives, if we will let the Holy Spirit be our Guide, we will find that He will lead us to places where we are most needed, instead of the places that we want to go.

As they passed by Mysia they came down to Troas, where Paul had a vision in the night. The thing he saw was a man of Macedonia, and he was saying "Come over into Macedonia and help us." The verse tells us that immediately after he had seen the vision they endeavored to go into Macedonia and the scripture tells us of their assurance of their call, "assuredly gathering that the Lord had called us for the preach the gospel unto them."

It was this verse as I stated earlier that the Lord used in calling me into the mission field. I was burdened and praying about going into Haiti to preach and the Lord gave me the assurance I needed to know that this is exactly what He wanted me and my family to do. We did deputation work for a while and made four mission trips there preaching the gospel with a group. We saw so many precious souls saved in these missionary journeys. On almost every trip, we saw a hundred are more souls saved in about a two week period of time. I praise the Lord for every opportunity that He gave us to preach the Gospel there and for every soul that was saved. Because of many circumstances that occurred, we were never able to go there and live, but the mission trips were what God wanted us to do at that time.

Paul and his mission team left Troas and went straight to Samothracia and the next day they came to Neapolis and from here they came to Philippi, which was the chief city in Macedonia. Paul tells us that they were in that city several days preaching. Thank God for Paul answering this call. Most of my ancestors came from Europe and here Paul is answering the call and preaching no doubt to some of my ancestors and hopefully many of them got saved. This, I believe, had a great deal to do with me being saved and preaching the gospel today.

DOWN BY THE RIVERSIDE

Acts 16:13 – 15 says, *"And on the sabbath we went out of the city by a river side, where prayer was wont to be made; and we sat down, and spake unto the women which resorted thither. 14 And a certain woman named Lydia, a seller of purple, of the city of Thyatira, which worshipped God, heard us: whose heart the Lord opened, that she attended unto the things which were spoken of Paul. 15 And when she was baptized, and her household, she besought us, saying, If ye have judged me to be faithful to the Lord, come into my house, and abide there. And she constrained us."*

It was from Philippi that they traveled out of the city on the sabbath and found a prayer meeting in a most unusual place, down by a river side. Paul and his team sat down with these women at the prayer meeting and began to speak to them. As they spoke there was a certain woman whose name was Lydia who heard them. When you preach or share the gospel message with people, you never know who might be listening to what you have to say. Lydia was a seller of purple from the city of Thyatira and she worshipped God. As she listened to them speak that day, the Lord opened her heart and she believed the things that were being said by Paul and got saved that day. Lydia was the first convert on their second missionary journey. She was so overcome by her new found faith that she was baptized there at the river and all of her household. This simply indicates that her family believed and were saved as well as Lydia and were baptized the same time she was.

Lydia then desires to have these men of God to come to her house and abide there. She uses the persuasion "If ye have judged me to be faithful" meaning that if you believe that I really got saved, then let me do this to show my sincerity for what you have done. She no doubt had plans to feed them and give them rest from their labors in Macedonia. One thing we should note in verse 15 is the last part where it says, "And she constrained us." Notice the word here "us". This was all the men of God that was with Paul at this point in his journey, which was Paul himself, Silas, Timothy and Luke. She "constrained" them to go, which means that she compelled or obliged them to go with her.

DELIVERANCE OF DAMSEL POSSESSED WITH A SPIRIT OF DIVINATION

Acts 16:16 – 22 says, "*And it came to pass, as we went to prayer, a certain damsel possessed with a spirit of divination met us, which brought her masters much gain by soothsaying: 17 The same followed Paul and us, and cried, saying, These men are the servants of the most high God, which shew unto us the way of salvation. 18 And this did she many days. But Paul, being grieved, turned and said to the spirit, I command thee in the name of Jesus Christ to come out of her. And he came out the same hour. 19 And when her masters saw that the hope of their gains was gone, they caught Paul and Silas, and drew them into the marketplace unto the rulers, 20 And brought them to the magistrates, saying, These men, being Jews, do exceedingly trouble our city, 21 And teach customs, which are not lawful for us to receive, neither to observe, being Romans. 22 And the multitude rose up together against them: and the magistrates rent off their clothes, and commanded to beat them.*"

Prayer was an important part of the life of Paul and those with him. We see them here again, going to pray. This should be a regular practice for the child of God. Notice when they came upon a prayer meeting by the river side, Lydia and her household were saved. Now they are coming to prayer and a certain damsel possessed with a spirit of divination met them, day after day. Her masters made a lot of money from her soothsaying. This lady is possessed by a devil and yet she has enough insight to say of Paul, Silas, Timothy and Luke in verse 17 that *"These men are the servants of the most high God, which shew unto us the way of salvation"*. She recognized the power of God working through them.

The Scripture tells us that she did this many days. Day after day as they were headed down to pray, this young lady would cry out as they passed by and Paul finally had enough and being grieved he turned and said to the spirit, "I command thee in the name of Jesus Christ to come out of her. And he came out of her that same hour." Dr. Sightler said, "the method I employ in casting out devils is to turn the light on, the light of the Gospel. When I preach the Gospel of the grace of God, the devils take leave and the devils flee because they despise the light, their deeds being evil." He further says, "Preachers and evangelist in our day have no apostolic authority to cast out devils as did Paul in this chapter."

When her masters saw what was done and that she had no more evil spirit in her to make money for them, they caught Paul and Silas and drew them into the marketplace to the rulers and magistrates and accused them. They said to them, "These men, being Jews, do exceedingly trouble our city, and teach customs, which are not lawful for us to receive or to observe because we are Romans." Notice the accusation is against who they are, Jews. This is definitely an anti-Semitic spirit. The people are persecuting them for being Jews, for being a part of the people of Israel. They accuse them of teaching things that they ought not, but again all they are doing is preaching the Gospel.

The multitude then rose up against Paul and Silas and the magistrates strip off their clothes and commanded them to be beaten. Paul and Silas did not deserve the punishment they were receiving. The only thing they had done was cast the devil out of this young lady and caused her masters to lose what money they were making from her.

PAUL AND SILAS BEATEN AND THROWN IN PRISON

Acts 16:23 – 34 tells us, "*And when they had laid many stripes upon them, they cast them into prison, charging the jailor to keep them safely: 24 Who, having received such a charge, thrust them into the inner prison, and made their feet fast in the stocks. 25 And at midnight Paul and Silas prayed, and sang praises unto God: and the prisoners heard them. 26 And suddenly there was a great earthquake, so that the foundations of the prison were shaken: and immediately all the doors were opened, and every one's bands were loosed. 27 And the keeper of the prison awaking out of his sleep, and seeing the prison doors open, he drew out his sword, and would have killed himself, supposing that the prisoners had been fled. 28 But Paul cried with a loud voice, saying, Do thyself no harm: for we are all here. 29 Then he called for a light, and sprang in, and came trembling, and fell down before Paul and Silas, 30 And brought them out, and said, Sirs, what must I do to be saved? 31 And they said, Believe on the Lord Jesus Christ, and thou shalt be saved, and thy house. 32 And they spake unto him the word of the Lord, and to all that were in his house. 33 And he took them the same hour of the night, and washed their stripes; and was baptized, he and all his, straightway. 34 And when he had brought them into his house, he set meat before them, and rejoiced, believing in God with all his house.*"

Along with the beating, which the Scripture refers to as "many stripes", they are then cast into prison. They are placed in charge of the jailer, who places them into the inner prison. Here are the two men of God, Paul and Silas, trying to follow the leading of the Holy Spirit, preaching the Word of God and doing the will of the Lord and yet they find themselves locked up in prison. Yes, bad things do happen to the children of God, but God has a way of turning the bad that happens in our lives into something good. He knows just how to use everything that happens to us to fulfill His will. Romans 8:28 says, *"And we know that all things work together for good to them that love God, to them who are the called according to his purpose."*

So with the charge against them of troubling the city, sowing discord and disturbing the public peace, they are beaten and cast into the inner prison for punishment. Remember it was Ahab that said to Elijah in 1 Kings 18:17, "Art thou he that troubleth Israel." Oh that we, as Christians, could trouble our cities and towns where we live." This troubling was the stirring of the message in the souls of men who would not hear. The shaking of the people that would have brought them peace forever, but they refused. Through our message and testimony many are troubled every day. God is working in their hearts and wanting them to receive the free gift He has for them through the grace given by Jesus Christ.

They are now in the "inner prison" which is the dungeon. A dark, damp, dreary place where only the worst criminals were placed. No doubt he thought that he could keep them from escaping if they were keep here. He put their feet in the stocks and locked them in. Here lies two men of God that have been wrongly accused, beaten with many stripes, suffering this punishment for the cause of Christ. Remember earlier when we mentioned the prayer life of Paul and Silas.

Well that has not changed. These men prayed about everything. Verse 25 tells us that *"And at midnight Paul and Silas prayed, and sang praises unto God: and the prisoners heard them."* They were not praying at an hour of prayer or in the house of prayer, but in a dungeon. There is no place or time when it is not a good time to pray!

Their hearts overflowed with the joy of their prayer. Wouldn't you like to have that prayer recorded in the scriptures? What did they say? What was their petition? Whatever it was, it stirred their hearts and here lying on a cold damp floor in pain and agony these men worshipped God. They may have been locked away, but God was right there with them. They felt His presence as they cried out to Him! Their hearts were so full of praise that they begin to sing. Oh what a time of worship these men had!

REVIVAL BREAKS OUT AT THE PRISON

But then something happened! Locked away in the innermost part of the prison, the other prisoners heard them. I believe they listened, many in unbelief and others wanting and longing for what these men of God had. Then another miracle happened. A great earthquake began to shake the prison and the very foundation of the prison was shaken. And immediately all the doors of the prison were opened and every one's bands were loosed. God heard their pray and God sent deliverance.

The keeper of the prisoners, being so sure that there was no way that any of these prisoners could ever escape, went to sleep. Probably the shaking of the earthquake and the sound of their chains falling off, along with the sound of the creaky doors of the prison being opened had awakened him. I believe that he was standing guard and then sleeping, just outside the door of the inner prison where Paul and Silas were being kept. When he woke up, he saw what had happened and supposing that everyone had escaped, drew out his sword to kill himself. The charge of the prisoners was on this jailer and if just one of the prisoners had escaped, the life of the jailer would be taken. He decided to miss all that and just go ahead and take his own life. But Paul cried out to him and said, "Do thyself no harm: for we are all here."

The jailer called for a light, remember it is so dark that you can't see your hand in front of your face, and then he ran in to where Paul and Silas were. There trembling, he fell down before them and the first thing he asked was "Sirs, what must I do to be saved?" They answered him by saying, "Believe on the Lord Jesus Christ, and thou shalt be saved, and thy house." Then they spoke unto him the Word of the Lord and to all those of his house. The keeper of the prison took them out of the prison and washed their stripes and then he and his whole household were baptized. That means that they got saved from hearing the message of Christ from Paul and Silas. The jailer then set them down and fed them all the while he was rejoicing, because he had put his trust in Christ. "Believing in God with all his house."

Though Paul and Silas were imprisoned and suffered wrongfully, the Lord worked it all out for His good and His glory. The jailers and his household got saved. Though that is all that Luke recorded about the events of that night, I believe that there were many of the prisoners, if not all of them, that got saved that night. I say that because when the opportunity for the prisoners to leave was provided, none of them left their cell. God knows what He is doing in every situation of life. All we need to do is just trust Him and continue to serve Him.

I also believe that the prison was rendered unusable, at least until it could be repaired, and it may never have been usable again. Several years ago when I was working in maintenance at an apartment complex, they had one whole section of the complex that was shut down due to a shift in the foundation. The outside doors and the inside doors as well would not open and close correctly, so they had to shut it down. I believe that something like this was possibly done to the prison that had held Paul and Silas.

PAUL AND SILAS LEAVE PRISON AND GO TO THE HOUSE OF LYDIA AND THEN DEPART

Acts 16:35 – 40 says, *"And when it was day, the magistrates sent the serjeants, saying, Let those men go. 36And the keeper of the prison told this saying to Paul, The magistrates have sent to let you go: now therefore depart, and go in peace. 37But Paul said unto them, They have beaten us openly uncondemned, being Romans, and have cast us into prison; and now do they thrust us out privily? nay verily; but let them come themselves and fetch us out. 38 And the serjeants told these words unto the magistrates: and they feared, when they heard that they were Romans. 39 And they came and besought them, and brought them out, and desired them to depart out of the city. 40 And they went out of the prison, and entered into the house of Lydia: and when they had seen the brethren, they comforted them, and departed."*

As soon as it was morning, the magistrates sent orders to let Paul and Silas go. Remember the magistrates had them beaten with many stripes publicly the day before. Now these same men that had beaten them are sent down to set them free. The jailer immediately tells Paul and Silas the news, *"The magistrates have sent to let you go, therefore depart, and go in peace."* Paul replies that they were beaten publicly and cast into prison and he also mentions that they were Romans. He tells the serjeants that if they want them out they will have to come and get them out themselves. The serjeants convey the message to the magistrates and immediately, fear grips there hearts in hearing that they were Romans. Matthew Henry says that "Roman historians give instances of cities that had their charters taken from them for indignities done to Roman citizens. Paul uses this later in Acts 22:25, 26. It did not bother them that they had beaten and imprisoned the servants of Christ. But fear filled their hearts to hear that they had done that to Roman citizens. They feared that someone would tell the government what they had done.

Paul refuses to leave until they acknowledge their injustice publicly. Then they came down themselves and brought them out of the prison and at the same time desired that they would depart out of the city. They left the prison and went to the house of Lydia where they knew they would be welcome. They had a final visit with the brethren, comforted them and then departed.

Paul and Silas had come to Philippi with a call and a burden, yet they saw little fruit of their labors and are now driven out of town. But they did not preach there in vain. Besides the account of Lydia and her household and the jailer and his household there was much sowing of seed in this place. Though they may not see it now, later they will see what great things they have done. The foundation of the church at Philippi was laid. The harvest shall come in due time.

NEXT STOP THESSALONICA

Acts 17:1 – 4 says, "*Now when they had passed through Amphipolis and Apollonia, they came to Thessalonica, where was a synagogue of the Jews: 2 And Paul, as his manner was, went in unto them, and three sabbath days reasoned with them out of the scriptures, 3 Opening and alleging, that Christ must needs have suffered, and risen again from the dead; and that this Jesus, whom I preach unto you, is Christ. 4 And some of them believed, and consorted with Paul and Silas; and of the devout Greeks a great multitude, and of the chief women not a few."*

Paul and Silas continue on in preaching the Word despite the treatment they receive in Philippi. He mentions this in his first letter to them in 1 Thessalonians 2:2 *"But even after that we had suffered before, and were shamefully entreated, as ye know, at Philippi, we were bold in our God to speak unto you the gospel of God with much contention."* The persecution and opposition that they met only made them more determined to get the gospel message out. That should be our desire. There will be those that will treat us in a bad way, but don't let that stop you from telling someone else about Christ.

Missions is not easy, but it's necessary. In His commission, He didn't say everyone would be receptive to the message, He only told us to go and tell them. He didn't say that people would love you because you told them the gospel message, but He did say go! At whatever the cost, Paul and Silas preached the word faithfully in every city and town they went into. We must be faithful in our witness.

Thessalonica was the chief city of this country. We're told that he only passed through Amphipolis which was a city near Philippi and Apollonia which was a city of Illyricum, near Thessalonica. Romans 15:19 says, *"Through mighty signs and wonders, by the power of the Spirit of God; so that from Jerusalem, and round about unto Illyricum, I have fully preached the gospel of Christ."* This indicates that in passing through these cities, He also took the time to preach the Gospel there.

In Thessalonica, he preach the gospel to the Jews first. Then for three sabbath days reasoned with them out of the scriptures. Notice how he reasoned, not from something he had been told nor from some thought someone had told him about Christ, but *"out of the scriptures."* He told them how that Christ "must needs have suffered and risen again from the dead" and then told them that this Jesus that he was preaching about was Christ or the Messiah. Most of the Jews had a hard time understanding the suffering of Christ, but Paul explains it was for us, for all men. He explains to them that Christ had to die in order to be resurrected for us.

The success of these three sabbath meetings was that *"some of them believed"*. Not only did they believe but they *"consorted with Paul and Silas."* A great multitude believed, yet there is no mention of the Gentile idolaters being preached to or getting saved. Yet we know that they did from Paul's letter to the church at Thessalonica in 1 Thess. 1:9 where he said, *"For they themselves shew of us what manner of entering in we had unto you, and how ye turned to God from idols to serve the living and true God;"*

Acts 17:5 – 9 says, *"But the Jews which believed not, moved with envy, took unto them certain lewd fellows of the baser sort, and gathered a company, and set all the city on an uproar, and assaulted the house of Jason, and sought to bring them out to the people. 6 And when they found them not, they drew Jason and certain brethren unto the rulers of the city, crying, These that have turned the world upside down are come hither also; 7 Whom Jason hath received: and these all do contrary to the decrees of Caesar, saying that there is another king, one Jesus. 8 And they troubled the people and the rulers of the city, when they heard these things. 9 And when they had taken security of Jason, and of the other, they let them go."*

In verse 5 we see the trouble that came from the great success of Paul and Silas in preaching the gospel and seeing so many saved. Wherever Paul and Silas preached they were sure to face opposition and persecution. They knew it was coming, but they preached anyhow. They were on a mission to tell people everywhere that they went, of the saving grace of Jesus. We are told here that the troublemakers were "*the Jews who believed not*" and notice they were "*moved with envy*". The Jews were usually the greatest enemies of Christianity. Paul mentioned this rage of the Jews in 1 Thess. 2: 15, 16 where he said, "*Who both killed the Lord Jesus, and their own prophets, and have persecuted us; and they please not God, and are contrary to all men: 16 Forbidding us to speak to the Gentiles that they might be saved, to fill up their sins alway: for the wrath is come upon them to the uttermost.*"

These Jews are said to have used certain lewd fellows of the baser sort. All the people who were wise treated Paul and Silas with respect, but this company of wicked men were glad to stand against them. Isn't it interesting that many times the troublemakers are the ones who just don't understand what Christianity is all about! These wicked, vile men are said to have "*set the city on an uproar.*" They basically started a riot. Matthew Henry says this is the way the devil carries on his designs: "he sets cities in an uproar, sets souls in an uproar, and then fishes in troubled waters." They assaulted the house of Jason, hoping to bring Paul and Silas out and no doubt pull them to pieces, but they could not find them.

Since they could not find Paul and Silas, they drew Jason out of his house and certain other brethren and brought them before the rulers of the city. Their accusation against them was "These that have turned the world upside down are come hither also." What an accusation! They are being accused of turning the world upside down. If you will be honest, that is exactly what happened when you got saved. Jesus coming into your heart rooted out the sin and washed it away! The way of the world that we were so accustomed to was turned upside down and we were a better people because of it. Actually, they were meaning to cause more trouble by this accusation, but they are telling the truth of what really happens when a person gets saved.

Another thought about this statement is that oh, that this could be made against us as believers today! That people would say about us, that we are turning the world upside down. Taking the message of the Gospel to a sinful people in love with the world and seeing them cleansed and walking away from the life style they once had in the world. They turn their accusations against Jason now saying that he has received these men.

In verse seven they give another accusation which is that "*these all do contrary to the decrees of Ceasar.*" They are not suggesting a certain law that was made, for there were none against Christianity, but they were saying what they were doing was against Ceasar's power. Notice they said, that Paul and Silas were preaching about another king, one Jesus. When Peter preached his first message to the Gentiles in Acts 10:36 he said, "*The word which God sent unto the children of Israel, preaching peace by Jesus Christ: (he is Lord of all:)*" The accusation carried no real force for Christ's kingdom was not of this world. They did not understand that when the Christians referred to Jesus as a King, they were not talking about one who was rival of Ceasar. Jesus even taught for men to "*render unto Ceasar the things that are Ceasar's.*"

The result of the accusations was that "*they troubled the people and the rulers of the city.*" When they heard that Paul and Silas were against Ceasar, they were troubled. They feared what might happen to them because of believing in and following the teaching of such men. Their hearts of both the people and the rulers of the city were troubled.

PAUL AND SILAS SENT TO BEREA

PAUL SENT TO ATHENS, SILAS AND TIMOTHY REMAIN IN BEREA

Acts 17:10 – 15 says, "*And the brethren immediately sent away Paul and Silas by night unto Berea: who coming thither went into the synagogue of the Jews. 11 These were more noble than those in Thessalonica, in that they received the word with all readiness of mind, and searched the scriptures daily, whether those things were so. 12 Therefore many of them believed; also of honourable women which were Greeks, and of men, not a few. 13 But when the Jews of Thessalonica had knowledge that the word of God was preached of Paul at Berea, they came thither also, and stirred up the people. 14 And then immediately the brethren sent away Paul to go as it were to the sea: but Silas and Timotheus abode there still. 15 And they that conducted Paul brought him unto Athens: and receiving a commandment unto Silas and Timotheus for to come to him with all speed, they departed.*"

The brethren, recognizing the danger that Paul and Silas were in, sent them by night to Berea. The first place they went to when they came into Berea was the Jewish synagogue. Dr. Sightler says the first place they always went was to the Jews. There are reasons for that he says. One of the reasons is because there were no Baptist churches or any other kind of churches, because the new church is now being founded upon the earth. Paul being a believer, went into the synagogue, for he was a Jew of the tribe of Benjamin, a Hebrew of the Hebrews. We are told that these were more noble than those in Thessalonica and the thing that made them this way was that they received the word with all readiness of mind and they searched the scriptures daily to see if what they were being taught and preached was the truth.

The people in Berea were more willing to listen to the preaching of Paul and Silas. They searched the scriptures to make sure they were being told the truth. They had an open mind to the word of God. Because of their willingness to search the scripture, they were more likely to find the truth that leads to eternal life. Dr. Sightler tells the story of the man who wrote the book Ben Hur, a man by the name of Lou Wallace. He was a Jew and when he began writing the book he was not a believer. But through all the daily research and reading and searching he did, by the time he had finished the book, he was a believer. "There is something about the Bible. It is the dynamite of God. It is the power of God unto salvation. The Bible is a living book; and when men read it, when men hear it, something happens, as surely as you live." Dr. Sightler

Because of their willingness to search the scriptures and these men of God preaching, verse 12 tells us than many of them believed. They were persuaded by the word of God that they needed Jesus and they repented and received Him as their Savior. We are told the many honorable women which were Greeks were saved and a good number of the men.

I always think when I come to this portion of Scripture, why those unbelieving Jews of Thessalonica never had any interest in those of Berea until they got saved. As soon as they knew about the great number of men and women that had been saved, they come to Berea with the sole purpose of stirring up the people. There will always be some who believe that their destiny on earth is to stir up some kind of trouble when God begins to move. This time the brethren in Berea send Paul away by sea. We are told that Silas and

Timothy remain there in Berea. Paul is brought by ship to Athens where he immediately sends for Silas and Timothy to come to Athens as soon as they can get there. 1 Thess. 3:1, 2 tells us that Timothy was sent by Thessalonica to check on their affairs and give a report to Paul. The Scripture here says, *"Wherefore when we could no longer forbear, we thought it good to be left at Athens alone; 2 And sent Timotheus, our brother, and minister of God, and our fellowlabourer in the gospel of Christ, to establish you, and to comfort you concerning your faith."*

PAUL ALONE AT ATHENS

Acts 17:16 – 34 says, *"Now while Paul waited for them at Athens, his spirit was stirred in him, when he saw the city wholly given to idolatry. 17 Therefore disputed he in the synagogue with the Jews, and with the devout persons, and in the market daily with them that met with him. 18 Then certain philosophers of the Epicureans, and of the Stoicks, encountered him. And some said, What will this babbler say? other some, He seemeth to be a setter forth of strange gods: because he preached unto them Jesus, and the resurrection. 19 And they took him, and brought him unto Areopagus, saying, May we know what this new doctrine, whereof thou speakest, is? 20 For thou bringest certain strange things to our ears: we would know therefore what these things mean. 21 (For all the Athenians and strangers which were there spent their time in nothing else, but either to tell, or to hear some new thing.) 22 Then Paul stood in the midst of Mars' hill, and said, Ye men of Athens, I perceive that in all things ye are too superstitious. 23 For as I passed by, and beheld your devotions, I found an altar with this inscription, TO THE UNKNOWN GOD. Whom therefore ye ignorantly worship, him declare I unto you. 24 God that made the world and all things therein, seeing that he is Lord of heaven and earth, dwelleth not in temples made with hands; 25 Neither is worshipped with men's hands, as though he needed any thing, seeing he giveth to all life, and breath, and all things; 26 And hath made of one blood all nations of men for to dwell on all the face of the earth, and hath determined the times before appointed, and the bounds of their habitation; 27 That they should seek the Lord, if haply they might feel after him, and find him, though he be not far from every one of us: 28 For in him we live, and move, and have our being; as certain also of your own poets have said, For we are also his offspring. 29 Forasmuch then as we are the offspring of God, we ought not to think that the Godhead is like unto gold, or silver, or stone, graven by art and man's device. 30 And the times of this ignorance God winked at; but now commandeth all men every where to repent: 31 Because he hath appointed a day, in the which he will judge the world in righteousness by that man whom he hath ordained; whereof he hath given assurance unto all men, in that he hath raised him from the dead. 32 And when they heard of the resurrection of the dead, some mocked: and others said, We will hear thee again of this matter. 33 So Paul departed from among them. 34 Howbeit certain men clave unto him, and believed: among the which was Dionysius the Areopagite, and a woman named Damaris, and others with them."*

The first impression that Paul has of Athens while he awaits the arrival of Silas and Timothy is expressed in the words *"his spirit was stirred in him, when he saw the city wholly given to idolatry."* Paul was not impressed at being in the great city of philosophy and learning. All he sees is a people that have replaced God with so many idols that they don't even know the true and living God. Therefore, he disputes with them about their condition. Remember Paul's mission wherever he is at is to preach the gospel message to those who are lost. He disputes (to engage in argument or debate) with the Jews in the synagogue, with the devout persons, (those showing deep religious feeling or commitment), with those in the market and those he meets along the way and he does it on a daily basis.

In verse 18 we are introduced to a group of philosophers who were of the Epicureans. The Epicureans, according to

Matthew Henry, were a group that viewed God as one as themselves, an idle inactive being, that did not put any difference between good and evil. They would not own, either that God made the world or that he governs it; nor that man needs to make any conscience of what he says or does, having no punishment to fear nor rewards to hope for. The Epicureans indulged themselves in all the pleasures of sense, and placed their happiness in them.

We are also introduced to the Stoicks who thought themselves to be as good as God and indulged themselves as much in the pride of life as the Epicureans did in the lusts of the flesh and of the eye. They taught contrary to Christianity which teaches us to deny ourselves and abase ourselves . . . that Christ may be all in all. These are the beliefs and lifestyles of these groups that "encountered him"

Many of these groups thought Paul to be a fool. They called him a babbler. *"What will this babbler say?"* The word "babbler" used by these philosophers meant "that he retailed odds and ends of knowledge which he had picked up from others, without possessing himself any system of thought or skill of language--without culture." Basically they were accusing him of doing what they were doing.

They also accused him of be a "setter forth of strange gods". This was because he had preached Jesus unto them and his resurrection. Though the philosophers in Athens were constantly seeking knowledge and were always interested in learning some new thing, the preaching and teaching of Paul concerning Jesus and His resurrection baffled them and they looked upon it as a strange doctrine.

They were so interested in knowing more about this Jesus and His resurrection that they brought Paul unto Areopagus or Mars Hill so that they might hear more about this new doctrine as they called it. They were interested in knowing what this doctrine was all about.

Paul then stood in the midst of Mars hill and said to those gathered there, *"Ye men of Athens, I perceive that in all things ye are too superstitious."* He states the reason for saying this to them was because of the devotion they had to the many idols throughout the city. They had an idol for every god they could think of, so as not to offend any of them.

The term *"too superstitious"* refers to a belief or practice resulting from ignorance, fear of the unknown, trust in magic or chance, or a false conception of causation. The idols that were everywhere in Athens was a good indicator. People today are altogether too superstitious and most of it comes from things we have been taught all our lives about what to do if a certain thing happens. But most of our "superstitions" come from a lack of knowledge of the Word of God. Knowing what God says and knowing what God has done with sin through His Son on Calvary helps to do away with a superstitious mind.

Some of the superstitions of today have been handed down for generations. Some of them are: Throwing salt over your shoulder, a black cat crossing your path, stepping on a crack, opening an umbrella indoors, a broken mirror, knocking on wood, a rabbits foot, a horseshoe, crossing your fingers, saying bless you when someone sneezes, sweeping under your feet, failing to respond to a chain letter, walking under a ladder, and many more! All of these, we have been told will either bring us luck or ward off evil spirits or bad luck from our lives. The truth is that none of them are true. If you are not completely sure, check with the Old King James Bible and see if you can find any truth to these old wives tales and superstitions that have been taught to us all our lives.

Paul, in continuing his message, says that he found and altar that was set up "*TO THE UNKNOWN GOD.*" That was just in case they had ignorantly forgotten one or left one off so that would cover all their bases in their so called worship. Paul then begins his message here using this altar that was set up to the Unknown God. He tells them that though they are ignorant of this God, "*Him declare I unto you.*"

Keep in mind that Paul is preaching the Gospel message here to heathen people. Those that do not know the true and living God and that are currently worshipping idols to gods that are not real. In teaching them what they were inquiring about it was necessary for Paul to lay a foundation. He tells them that His God is the One who created all things; that created the world and being the Lord of heaven and of earth, needed not to dwell in temples made by men. He says that God is not worshipped by men's hands, for God has given to every man, life and breath and all things. God has created and is concerned with the lives of all men. He has set bounds for their habitation.

He then says, in verse 27, "*That they should seek the Lord, if haply they might feel after him, and find him, though he be not far from every one of us:*" Paul is telling them that God is everywhere present and He has his eye on us at all times and knows us better than we know ourselves. He is near you, yet because of unbelief, so far away from you. He continues his message by telling them that it is in him we live and move and have our being. He is saying that we have a necessary dependence on Him. He uses the saying that we are His offspring, which refers to the fact we are formed by Him, formed for him and have more care from Him than any parent has ever cared for their child.

Because we are His offspring, we ought not to think of the Godhead as an idol, made of gold or silver or stone carved out by some man's hand. Paul then turns his message toward an invitation where he preaches to them that God commandeth that all men everywhere repent. There will be a day of judgment he says when God will judge the world in Righteousness, by the one He has ordained, Jesus, and then he tells them that God gave the assurance to men by raising Him from the dead.

As he mentions the resurrection, some of them mocked him. Others said to him, we will hear thee again concerning what you have said. Then there were also those who clave to him and believed. That is usually the way a message on Jesus will turn out. Some will mock in unbelief; others will say, that may be so, but we will have to hear more; and others will believe and want to know more about the Lord. We are given some of those who clave to him here, *"Dionysius the Areopagite, and a woman named Damaris, and others with them."* Though the harvest at Athens was not as great as at other places Paul had been, he could not leave this place saying that he had labored here in vain.

PAUL GOES TO CORINTH

Acts 18:1-6 says, *"After these things Paul departed from Athens, and came to Corinth; 2 And found a certain Jew named Aquila, born in Pontus, lately come from Italy, with his wife Priscilla; (because that Claudius had commanded all Jews to depart from Rome:) and came unto them. 3 And because he was of the same craft, he abode with them, and wrought: for by their occupation they were tentmakers. 4 And he reasoned in the synagogue every sabbath, and persuaded the Jews and the Greeks. 5 And when Silas and Timotheus were come from Macedonia, Paul was pressed in the spirit, and testified to the Jews that Jesus was Christ. 6 And when they opposed themselves, and blasphemed, he shook his raiment, and said unto them, Your blood be upon your*

own heads; I am clean: from henceforth I will go unto the
Gentiles."

Though Paul's reception at Athens had not been with
persecutions as he had faced in other places in dealing with
the Jews where they has run him out of the city, yet the
reception was cold. He departs from Athens on his own
leaving the care of these new converts to Dionysius, and
travels to Corinth. It is here at Corinth, the chief city of
Achaia, a rich and splendid city, a seacoast village on the
Aegean Sea, that Paul is instrumental in establishing a
church.

It is at Corinth that Paul finds a Jewish man named
Aquila and his wife, Priscilla. They had come here to Corinth
because of Claudius, the Roman Caesar. He hated the Jews
and expelled them from Rome until they were all gone.
Aquila and Priscilla had to leave and came to Athens, Greece
and from there had come up to Corinth. Isn't it amazing
how God works in people's lives? Even though the
persecution was bad and they had to leave their home, had it
not been for this, Paul would never have been able to meet
them and use them in the ministry. What a wonderful God
we serve!

Paul, along with Priscilla and Aquila, were tent makers.
So he worked with them while he was in Corinth. In these
days tents were quite common. Dr. Sightler said, "The
thought occurred to me, I wonder how and why and when
Paul became interested in building tents. As far as I know,
there is not ever the remotest suggestion in all Paul's epistle
as to why and how he became involved in this craft. It could
have well been his father was a tentmaker, or it could have
been that he had a brother or somebody else in his family
who might have been a tentmaker. It could have been his
grandfather might have been a tentmaker. For some reason,

Paul learned the art. So far as I am concerned, Paul was not only a tentmaker; but he was a trained educated man, a man of renown who sat at the feet of Gamaliel. And yet he had this craft which he could always fall back on to make a livelihood."

Paul, in verse 4, is doing exactly what he has done in all the other cities he had visited. The first thing he does is find the synagogue and on the Sabbath day he goes here to persuade and reason and preach and proclaim a resurrected Savior. This he does every Sabbath without exception.

We see that Silas and Timothy once again join the team in Corinth. They had stayed behind in Berea when Paul had to leave for his safety. Paul waited in Athens for them to join him, but they never came. Now they arrive from Berea and are ready to begin work here. The scripture tells us that when they came, Paul was *"pressed in the spirit."* This means that he was burdened in his heart and had a consuming desire to preach the gospel to the Corinthians. This is just what he did, we are told he testified to them that "Jesus was Christ". He tells them that the Jesus he is preaching was the Messiah.

The Jews would not readily believe this, but the Gentiles believed. "When they opposed themselves, and blasphemed" meaning when they contradicted in their lives what they put their faith in, Paul then shook his raiment and said, "Your blood be upon your own heads." The Jews and the Greeks had rejected the message of the resurrection of Jesus and the message that Jesus was the Messiah. Paul tells them that he has preached daily to them about Christ, yet they will not accept this truth, so he declares that he is clean from their blood. He had done what he was sent to do, but they would not have the message that was sent, so Paul again says here that he will go unto the Gentiles.

So many times when we preach or teach or tell others about Jesus, the message falls on ground where the seed is never going to grow. Time after time, we tell them and time after time they turn us away. This is the way Paul was feeling at this time. He had preached faithfully, but for the most part his message was falling on deaf ears. They would not accept the truth of what Paul was preaching, but he never gave up.

Acts 18:7 – 11 says, *"And he departed thence, and entered into a certain man's house, named Justus, one that worshipped God, whose house joined hard to the synagogue. 8 And Crispus, the chief ruler of the synagogue, believed on the Lord with all his house; and many of the Corinthians hearing believed, and were baptized. 9 Then spake the Lord to Paul in the night by a vision, Be not afraid, but speak, and hold not thy peace: 10 For I am with thee, and no man shall set on thee to hurt thee: for I have much people in this city. 11 And he continued there a year and six months, teaching the word of God among them."*

Paul leaves the synagogue here because of the unbelieving Jews and comes to the house of a man by the name of Justus. It would seem that Justus, living close to the synagogue had opened his doors so that Paul could continue preaching the gospel. We are told that Justus worshipped God. He was not an idol worshipper, but he was a Gentile. His house being close to the synagogue made it possible for some from the synagogue to come in to the meeting Paul was having.

Paul had results here that he probably had not expected. We are told that Crispus, who was the chief ruler of the synagogue had come and heard the message and had believed on the Lord Jesus Christ. Not only had he gotten saved, but all his house had believed. Also there were many

Corinthians who heard the message and believed and were baptized. God continues to bless Paul with converts even though the Jews at the synagogue had rejected his message.

Paul, then in a vision at night, is told by the Lord, "Be not afraid, but speak, and hold not thy peace." Just keep on preaching the Word. Don't ever give up!

Preach on, don't give up, so many need to hear.
Preach on, Preach on, their faces never fear.
Preach on, take a stand, tell them what is right.
Preach on, Preach on, be faithful in the fight.

Then the Lord gave him a promise of protection. He needed not to fear man, because God had promised to be with him and shield him from wicked and ungodly attacks. We have a similar promise in our commission to take the gospel message to the lost in Matthew 28:20 ". . . and, lo, I am with you alway, even unto the end of the world."

God was giving great victory to his servant Paul. People were getting saved. The Lord gave him a promise and also told him that He had much people in the city. Paul's journeys, up until now, have been moving at a pretty rapid pace. But, in Corinth, he stays here for a year and six months teaching the word of God among them. It was during this time that Paul won a great number of the people of Corinth to the Lord. It was here he built a church that we read more about in 1 and 2 Corinthians. He never gave up and God rewarded him with results. His faithfulness should teach us. Dr. Sightler says, "We ought to learn the lesson of consistency, the lesson of faithfulness, the lesson of doing what God wills we do, and being what God wills we be."

PAUL FINISHES THE JOURNEY

Acts 18:12 – 17 says, "*And when Gallio was the deputy of Achaia, the Jews made insurrection with one accord against Paul, and brought him to the judgment seat, 13 Saying, This fellow persuadeth men to worship God contrary to the law. 14 And when Paul was now about to open his mouth, Gallio said unto the Jews, If it were a matter of wrong or wicked lewdness, O ye Jews, reason would that I should bear with you: 15 But if it be a question of words and names, and of your law, look ye to it; for I will be no judge of such matters. 16 And he drave them from the judgment seat. 17 Then all the Greeks took Sosthenes, the chief ruler of the synagogue, and beat him before the judgment seat. And Gallio cared for none of those things.*"

It is always just a matter of time before Paul faces persecution from unbelievers when he travels on his missionary journeys. We should learn a lesson here as well, that if we are faithful to preach and teach and tell others the truth of the gospel, we too will face persecution. 2 Timothy 3:12 says, "*Yea, and all that will live godly in Christ Jesus shall suffer persecution.*" If you live a godly life before this lost world, you will suffer persecution. Get used to it. It's going to happen. When it does, don't quit doing what you are supposed to be doing. Keep on being faithful to the Lord.

Here we are introduced to one Gallio who was the deputy of Achaia. That means that he was a judge in the city of Corinth. It was during his time in office that the Jews made insurrection with one accord against Paul. Insurrection is "a violent uprising against an authority." They then brought him to the judgment seat and accused him of persuading men to worship God contrary to the law. Which statement was true! Paul's message was contrary to the law. He had a greater faith to teach. He had a message that was for all that would hear and receive to take of the water of eternal life freely.

As Paul has heard the accusations against him, he is about to defend himself when Gallio stops him and addresses the Jews that brought him there. He tells them that if the matter before him is one of wrong or lewdness, he would gladly hear it. But he tells them if it is something that has to do with their law, you take care of it. He tells them that he will not judge in spiritual matters and with that he ran them out from the judgment seat.

The Greeks then out of revenge, take Sosthenes, who was the chief ruler of the synagogue and beat him before the judgment seat. Then the scriptures tell us, "*And Gallio cared for none of these things.*" In other words, Gallio allowed this to happen. There was no reason for this to happen, but it did. Gallio was right in not judging Paul, but he is absolutely wrong for not stepping in and stopping this injustice against Sosthenes.

Acts 18:18 – 22, "*And Paul after this tarried there yet a good while, and then took his leave of the brethren, and sailed thence into Syria, and with him Priscilla and Aquila; having shorn his head in Cenchrea: for he had a vow. 19 And he came to Ephesus, and left them there: but he himself entered into the synagogue, and reasoned with the Jews. 20 When they desired him to tarry longer time with them, he consented not; 21 But bade them farewell, saying, I must by all means keep this feast that cometh in Jerusalem: but I will return again unto you, if God will. And he sailed from Ephesus. 22 And when he had landed at Caesarea, and gone up, and saluted the church, he went down to Antioch.*"

Paul tarried yet a good while here and then left and sailed to Syria. He took Priscilla and Aquila with him. The reason for his head being shorn and the vow he made in Cenchrea is not known. Dr. Sightler says, "The only explanation I can give as to Paul's deed and Paul's conduct was his consuming compassion for his kinsmen according to the flesh, and his longing desire to reach them with the Gospel of the grace of God."

Paul then left this port city, Cenchrea and came to Ephesus. We are told that at Ephesus he left Priscilla and Aquila. Paul continued to reason with the Jews in the synagogue. They wanted him to stay longer, but he was determined to keep the feast in Jerusalem. He promises them that he will visit them again and then adds, "*if God will.*" Matthew Henry says, "Our times are in God's hand; we purpose, but he disposes; and therefore we must make all our promise with submission to the will of God."

He sailed from Ephesus and landed in Caesarea and went up and saluted the church in Jerusalem. He was there only briefly. Then he went down to Antioch. Here he would again rehearse the mission journey and what had happened to his sending church. It no doubt was a refreshing time for Paul to be able to see his friends and brethren again.

Paul's Third Missionary Journey

THE WAY OF GOD MORE PERFFECTLY

Acts 18: 23 says, *"And after he had spent some time there, he departed, and went over all the country of Galatia and Phrygia in order, strengthening all the disciples."*

The thing on Paul's heart was to visit the brethren in Galatia and Phrygia where he had already been and to strengthen them. It is an important thing for the minister to realize the ministry of edifying the believers or strengthening them with the word. Dr. Sightler said that, "our preaching and fellowship and our doctrine and our methods and our pattern of service ought to be so as to strengthen and so as to encourage and so as to edify the body of Christ. . . It is the responsibility of every man of God to strengthen all the disciples."

Acts 18:24 – 28, *"And a certain Jew named Apollos, born at Alexandria, an eloquent man, and mighty in the scriptures, came to Ephesus. 25 This man was instructed in the way of the Lord; and being fervent in the spirit, he spake and taught diligently the things of the Lord, knowing only the baptism of John. 26 And he began to speak boldly in the synagogue: whom when Aquila and Priscilla had heard, they took him unto them, and expounded unto him the way of God more perfectly. 27 And when he was disposed to pass into Achaia, the brethren wrote, exhorting the disciples to receive him: who, when he was come, helped them much which had believed through grace: 28 For he mightily convinced the Jews, and that publickly, shewing by the scriptures that Jesus was Christ."*

In verse 24 we are introduced to a man by the name of Apollos. He had come to Ephesus when Paul had departed back in verse 21. We are told that he was a Jew, that he was born in Alexandria, which we understand to be in Egypt, and that he was an eloquent man. "Eloquent" means that he was able to express himself clearly and well. Verse 24 tells us that he was "mighty in the scriptures." This means that he was well versed in the word of God. Matthew Henry says that he "understood the sense and meaning of them, he knew how to make use of them and to apply them, how to reason out of the scriptures, and to reason strongly; a convincing, commanding, confirming power went along with all his expositions and applications of the scripture." He was "instructed in the way of the Lord", meaning he had been taught how a person is to put faith in Christ and to get saved. We are also told that he was "fervent in the spirit". The word "fervent" means to have intense feeling and enthusiasm for something. It is also said to be "hot, burning or glowing".

Apollos was a man "fervent" on fire, with the spirit of God on him. He was a preacher that people listened to when he preached. He was a man that many, no doubt, would come to hear him, just to watch him burn. Yet the Bible here tells us that he only knew of the baptism of John. Henry says that, "We cannot but think he had heard of Christ's death and resurrection, but he was not let into the mystery of them, had not had opportunity of conversing with any of the apostles since the pouring out of the Spirit; or he had himself been baptized only with the baptism of John, but was not baptized with the Holy Ghost, as the disciples were at the day of Pentecost."

Dr. Sightler says concerning this term used "knowing only the baptism of John", which is to say he did not fully know that which our Lord had done in turning to the Gentiles, and preaching to the Gentiles and receiving the Gentiles on and equal basis with the Jew.

Matthew Henry also tells us "He was a lively affectionate preacher; as he had a good head, so he had a good heart; he was fervent in Spirit. He had in him a great deal of divine fire as well as divine light, was burning as well as shining. He was full of zeal for the glory of God, and the salvation of precious souls."

He spoke boldly in the synagogue and when Aquila and Priscilla heard him, they took him into their house and expounded unto him the way of God more perfectly. Was he not God's man? Was he not preaching the Word of God? Was he not holding the attention of the people as they listened to him? The answer to all these questions, of course, is yes. But sometimes God will allow others to help you see things in a clearer way. That was the "expounding" work of Aquila and Priscilla. They understood more about some of the things that he needed to know and they took the time to teach the man of God. Aquila had a great knowledge of the word of God, but he never tried to preach in the synagogue because he didn't have the ability that Apollos had in his eloquent speech and delivery of the message to the people. But in Christian love, Aquila and Priscilla taught him things that would not only help him, but would help those that heard him.

In verse 27 it tells us that he did not receive a call to go to Achaia as Paul had, nor did he have an invitation to come there, but that he was "disposed" to pass into Achaia. This word "disposed" means to give a tendency to: incline. He heard of the state of the churches there and he had a mind to try to help them. God had disposed his mind to go. His friends encouraged him to go and approved by giving him letters of recommendation, urging the people of Achaia to receive him. We are told that when he came that he helped them much which had believed through grace. He instructed and preached to the Christians there and no doubt, showed them "the way of God more perfectly". This is an important part of ministry that many have forgotten. He took the time to build the Christians there up in the faith they had in Christ. We need to remember that those who are saved need preaching as well as those that are lost. Teach them, instruct them, convince them and compel them to find and walk in the perfect will of God for their lives.

Another lesson we can learn from Apollos here is that in finding the "mission field" he needed to work in, his desire was to go where he could help people. The burden of his heart was to teach the Christians here and preach Christ to those that did not know Him. That should be our desire in finding the will of God for our lives.

His message when he came into Achaia was to preach Christ and to convince the Jews that Jesus was the Messiah. He showed them from the scriptures daily, that Jesus was Christ. This resulted in many being convinced and putting their trust in Jesus Christ.

HAVE YOU RECEIVED THE HOLY GHOST

Acts 19:1 – 7 says, "*And it came to pass, that, while Apollos was at Corinth, Paul having passed through the upper coasts came to Ephesus: and finding certain disciples, 2 He said unto them, Have ye received the Holy Ghost since ye believed? And they said unto him, We have not so much as heard whether there be any Holy Ghost. 3 And he said unto them, Unto what then were ye baptized? And they said, Unto John's baptism. 4 Then said Paul, John verily baptized with the baptism of repentance, saying unto the people, that they should believe on him which should come after him, that is, on Christ Jesus. 5 When they heard this, they were baptized in the name of the Lord Jesus. 6 And when Paul had laid his hands upon them, the Holy Ghost came on them; and they spake with tongues, and prophesied. 7 And all the men were about twelve."*

While Apollos was preaching at Corinth, Paul was passing through the upper coasts and came to Ephesus. It was here that he found "certain" disciples, they are not named, but are mentioned as "disciples" meaning they were followers of the Lord Jesus. He asks these disciples a question, *"Have ye received the Holy Ghost since ye believed."* We should, as believers today, have an answer for that question. Dr. Sightler said that in our day, the church age, it takes place at the moment of conversion. We are born of the Spirit, baptized of the Spirit into the body of Christ; and every believer receives the Holy Spirit at the moment you are born again. The idea you get converted at a point and then in some other day, you receive the Holy Ghost, is not taught in the holy Scriptures at all. And neither does this verse teach such either.

It would be good for us to understand what Paul was asking and then ask ourselves the same question. Have we received the Holy Ghost since we believed? Matthew Henry says, "The tree will be known by the fruits of the Spirit. Do we bring forth the fruits of the Spirit? Are we led by the Spirit? Do we walk in the Spirit? Are we under the government of the Spirit?"

They did not pretend to know what Paul was talking about and readily acknowledged their ignorance. "We have not so much as heard whether there be any Holy Ghost." Paul thought this to be strange that they did not know and then asks them another question, "Unto what then were ye baptized?" Matthew Henry said, "Ignorance of the Holy Ghost is as inconsistent with a sincere profession of Christianity as ignorance of Christ is." Their answer was that they were baptized unto John's baptism.

Dr. Sightler asks, "Has it ever occurred to you the only baptism my Lord ever had was the baptism of John. . . The only baptism so far as the Bible is concerned that Matthew and John and Peter and James and all the twelve apostles of our Lord had was the baptism of John." He points out that the "baptism of John" was a good thing and a godly thing and there is no fault, there is nothing wrong with John's baptism. John's baptism had to do with the Jew and the old covenant. John's baptism is not related at all to the church or to converts after the Day of Pentecost, when the church was initiated.

These twelve disciples that Paul questions here had a good baptism, but it was related to the old covenant. It did not relate to Christian baptism. Dr. Sightler further tells us that John's baptism is a peculiar experience of a transitional period for the Jews and Jewish proselytes only. There is no record in the New Testament where John the Baptist, ever baptized even one Gentile.

When we study the book of Acts, we need to remember that it is not a book we use to teach doctrine. That is not the purpose of Luke writing this book. It is a transitional book. This is a book showing the Holy Spirit's working in the hearts of believers in a transition from Judaism to Christianity. We can learn many things from Acts, but must remember that is was not given to teach doctrine to the church. We learn the moving and working of the Holy Spirit and those that were led by the Spirit and what He did through them and by them. That being said, Paul teaches these believers here that John's baptism was not only showing a repentance or a turning away from sin, but also pointing to Christ and His finished work on Calvary. For this reason, Paul either baptizes them or has them baptized in "the name of the Lord Jesus".

That is not the formula for baptism that is given in Matthew 28:19 where it says, "Go ye therefore, and teach all nations, baptizing them in the name of the Father, and of the Son, and of the Holy Ghost:" Verse 5 here in chapter 19 is the same baptism that Peter commanded of the Jews at the Day of Pentecost where he said, "Repent and be baptized every one of you, in the name of Jesus Christ." This is not the baptism for the church age. The Jews are given this at Pentecost to identify them with the very one whom they crucified, rejected and had put to death. In the church age, we are to baptize in the name of a Triune God. This baptismal formula is given with the commission to the church.

Then Paul does something else that is not done in the Church Age. He laid his hands upon them. We have a lot of this being done, but is it for the Church? The age of the apostles shows us that they had apostolic authority by lay on of hands to be able to impart the Holy Spirit to anyone whom they desired to. We see it in several places in the book of Acts. We saw it in Caesarea in the days of Philip the evangelist. We see it in John and Peter and others. But we do not see it in our day.

The result was that all the men began to speak with tongues as they did on the day of Pentecost in Acts 2. They begin to preach and to prophesy. They were preaching in the power and fervency of the Holy Spirit. Oh, that we had men that would do this today! We need men filled with the Holy Spirit, set on fire with the fervency of the Spirit going forth and telling men and women and boys and girls about Jesus. What a difference it would make! So many are trying to do this in their own power and according to their own ability and it just will not work.

ALL WHICH DWELL IN ASIA

Acts 19: 8 – 12 says, *"And he went into the synagogue, and spake boldly for the space of three months, disputing and persuading the things concerning the kingdom of God. 9 But when divers were hardened, and believed not, but spake evil of that way before the multitude, he departed from them, and separated the disciples, disputing daily in the school of one Tyrannus. 10 And this continued by the space of two years; so that all they which dwelt in Asia heard the word of the Lord Jesus, both Jews and Greeks. 11 And God wrought special miracles by the hands of Paul: 12 So that from his body were brought unto the sick handkerchiefs or aprons, and the diseases departed from them, and the evil spirits went out of them."*

Paul continues to do what he has done elsewhere in preaching and teaching in the synagogue and we are told that he did this for about three months. One thing here in this verse that jumped out at me was the fact that Paul did this disputing and persuading through his preaching "boldly". He was not trying to hide or to do it secretly. He wanted them to know that he was not ashamed of the Christ that he taught and preached. We need to get a backbone, spiritually, about us when we are telling others about Jesus. There is no reason to be timid and appear to be ashamed of Him and what He has done for us.

Paul preached to them the things concerning the kingdom of God. The "kingdom of God" is used 68 times in the New Testament. The phrase "the kingdom of heaven" is used only 32 times and all in the book of Matthew. According to Scofield, the kingdom of heaven "signifies the Messianic earth rule of Jesus Christ, the Son of David."

In Scofield's notes on Matthew 6:33, he states that the kingdom of God can be distinguished from the kingdom of heaven in five respects. The characteristics of the kingdom of God are summarized as follows:

The Kingdom Of God Is Universal and Includes Angels and Saints Of All Ages.

The Kingdom Of God Is Entered Only By The New Birth.

The Kingdom Of God And The Kingdom Of Heaven Have Almost All Things In Common.

The Kingdom Of God Is Chiefly Inward And Spiritual.

The Kingdom Of God Merges Into The Kingdom Of Heaven When Christ Puts All Things Under His Feet.

W. E. Vine in his "Concise Dictionary of the Bible" says on page 208 that "God" is not the equivalent of "the heavens." He is everywhere and above all dispensations, whereas "the heavens" are distinguished from the earth, until the Kingdom comes in judgment and power and glory Rev. 11:15 when rule in heaven and on earth will be one.

Thus Paul preached concerning the kingdom of God and never once mention the kingdom of Heaven. We see that, as he preached, he did so first in showing them their obligations to God. He then preached to them argumentatively, he disputed. He took the scriptures and showed them where they were wrong in their beliefs. He also preached affectionately, he persuaded them. He preached in such a way as that no one could doubt or deny that he was right according to the scriptures.

The next verse tells us the two things that preaching the gospel will do. It will either soften your heart to receive it or it will harden you heart to reject it. This is what we see here. "When divers were hardened" we're told, they believed not but spoke evil of the way that Paul was preaching. Dr. Sightler said that "When a man hears the Gospel, it either draws him to God or drives him further away. Paul had been preaching in Ephesus for 3 months this same message concerning Jesus and now those that are hardened and believed not want to cause trouble. The problem was so severe that Paul departed from them and separated the believers from that crowd of unbelievers. We are not to be yoked together with unbelievers so Paul fixes the problem so that the believers and unbelievers are not having communion or fellowship. This takes care of the problem of being influenced by the lies of those that will not hold to the truths of the Word of God.

Paul began preaching and disputing then in the school of one by the name of Tyrannus. We are told he continued preaching here for two years. A statement is then made that should shame every Christian that has never told anyone about Jesus. It says, *"so that all they which dwell in Asia heard the word of the Lord Jesus, both Jews and Greeks."* All the people heard about Jesus through the preaching of Paul. How we ought to be diligent to get the message of Christ and His salvation offered to man out to this lost and dying world. What are you doing to help further the message?

Then we are told that "God wrought special miracles by the hands of Paul". God did this through Paul because he was an apostle. Dr. Sightler said, "And being an apostle he had a special apostolic gift and apostolic power to perform many kinds of miracles." The miracle is described telling us that from Paul's body were brought handkerchiefs or aprons and placed on the bodies of the sick and the diseases departed from them and the evil spirits went out of them.

Some still believe that in our day that we can do the same, but this was only done through apostolic power that God allowed through Paul. Dr. Sightler says there were only 12 apostles named in Matthew 10 and Paul took the place of Judas Iscariot. These men had apostolic power and apostolic authority which no man has today. When the last apostle died the apostolic miracles ceased. This is not the way of healing in our day. James 5 is the way of healing in our day. The healing was done through the miracles that God wrought by the hands of Paul. It was not the handkerchiefs that healed, it was the power of the Spirit of God.

MIGHTLY GREW THE WORD OF GOD

Acts 19: 13 – 20 says, *"Then certain of the vagabond Jews, exorcists, took upon them to call over them which had evil spirits the name of the Lord Jesus, saying, We adjure you by Jesus whom Paul preacheth. 14 And there were seven sons of one Sceva, a Jew, and chief of the priests, which did so. 15 And the evil spirit answered and said, Jesus I know, and Paul I know; but who are ye? 16 And the man in whom the evil spirit was leaped on them, and overcame them, and prevailed against them, so that they fled out of that house naked and wounded. 17 And this was known to all the Jews and Greeks also dwelling at Ephesus; and fear fell on them all, and the name of the Lord Jesus was magnified. 18 And many that believed came, and confessed, and shewed their deeds. 19 Many of them also which used curious arts brought their books together, and burned them before all men: and they counted the price of them, and found it fifty thousand pieces of silver. 20 So mightily grew the word of God and prevailed."*

In verse 13 we see some of the vagabond (wandering) Jews who tried to imitate the authority and power God had given Paul and we see the tragedy that comes through trying to imitate the power of God. They were said to be "exorcists" which is defined as "a person who expels or attempts to expel a supposed evil spirit from a person or place." That's what they were attempting to do. They urged them or adjured them by Jesus whom Paul preached.

In verse 14 we are introduced to the seven sons of Sceva. Sceva was a Jew and the chief priest. These sons attempted to imitate the miracles that Paul had performed through his apostolic powers. As they were trying to cast out an evil spirit, in verse 15, we are told," *the evil spirit answered and said, Jesus I know, and Paul I know; but who are ye? And the man in whom the evil spirit was leaped on them (these seven sons) and overcame them.*" One man, filled with and evil spirit, took on seven men and overcame them. He says that they prevailed against them and they fled from the house "naked and wounded." Don't try to imitate the miracles wrought by the apostles!

When this was known to the Jews and Greeks, great fear fell on them all and the name of Jesus was magnified. The imitators were exposed as frauds, but instead of hindering the work, the Lord was glorified and magnified more than before.

This caused a bit of a Revival among the believers in that they came and confessed and shewed their deeds. To show their repentance for their deeds, many of them that were involved in the curious arts, brought the books that were teaching them the wrong things and burned them there. We are told that they burned fifty thousand pieces of silver worth of books. What were these books? No doubt they were books they were using that was teaching them things about magic and divination. They probably were books that contained astrology, fortune telling, things dealing with spirits, the telling of the future and maybe even some of their plays, and romance books and love stories. It would do us good to go through some of our literature and get rid of some of the things that we shouldn't have or read in the first place. If you really want to read, the most intriguing book you can read will be the Word of God. The Bible will teach us and instruct us and guide us in the right way we should live. These believers recognized the things they were doing was wrong and repented of them and got rid of the things that would lead them away from God.

They were showing that they never intended to go back to this again and so burned the books that were leading them astray. They could have just taken them down from the shelves and put them in a box and put them away somewhere that they wouldn't readily have them at hand, but they were through with these forever, so they burned them. When we repent of sin in our lives, the best way to make sure we don't continue in that sin or go back to that sin is to remove the temptation from us completely.

We then read that the results and progress of the gospel in Ephesus is this, "*So mightily grew the word of God and prevailed.*" It grew mightily in that many were added to the church. The people saw that what these believers had was real and they wanted to be a part of and participate in what they had. The grace of God is seen in these believers in that they showed their faith by taking a strong stand against things that were displeasing to God and that would cause them to stray from Him.

Acts 19:21-23 says, "*After these things were ended, Paul purposed in the spirit, when he had passed through Macedonia and Achaia, to go to Jerusalem, saying, After I have been there, I must also see Rome. 22 So he sent into Macedonia two of them that ministered unto him, Timotheus and Erastus; but he himself stayed in Asia for a season. 23 And the same time there arose no small stir about that way.*"

We see that Paul is making plans here to further the gospel. He has been called to carry the gospel message to others and so he decides in his heart what he is going to do. He decides that when they passes through Macedonia and Achaia that he will go to Jerusalem and afterward, he would go to Rome. He sent Timotheus and Erastus ahead to Macedonia and planned to join them later. Paul stayed in Asia for a while and while he was there another conflict arose because of the things Paul was preaching. The Scripture says, *"no small stir about the way"*. This is, as Dr. Sightler says, the way of faith, the way of the Gospel, the way Paul had faithfully been preaching in the city of Ephesus. And that "way" that he was preaching was the way of Jesus, the way of the cross, the way of faith, the way of repentance.

THE TEMPLE OF DIANA

Acts. 19:24 – 28 says, *"For a certain man named Demetrius, a silversmith, which made silver shrines for Diana, brought no small gain unto the craftsmen; 25 Whom he called together with the workmen of like occupation, and said, Sirs, ye know that by this craft we have our wealth. 26 Moreover ye see and hear, that not alone at Ephesus, but almost throughout all Asia, this Paul hath persuaded and turned away much people, saying that they be no gods, which are made with hands: 27 So that not only this our craft is in danger to be set at nought; but also that the temple of the great goddess Diana should be despised, and her magnificence should be destroyed, whom all Asia and the world worshippeth. 28 And when they heard these sayings, they were full of wrath, and cried out, saying, Great is Diana of the Ephesians."*

The conflict was caused by a man by the name of Demetrius who was a silversmith. He was the one who made the silver shrines for Diana which was bringing in a lot of money. In Ephesus these silver shrines or idols, were used by many to worship Diana. Demetrius calls all the other workmen together as he is concerned that they are about to be put out of business by Paul's preaching and makes accusation against him. Notice how he address him where he refers to him as "This Paul". The accusation was that Paul had caused man to understand how wrong this idol worship was and caused them to turn away from these idols. Many, no doubt, destroyed these idols to completely remove them from their lives. Basically they are saying that Paul's preaching is bad for business. He is causing us to lose money.

In verse 27 we see just how much influence the worship of Diana had on the people of Ephesus. "The Temple of Diana was supported by 127 Ionic columns, each towering 60 feet tall, it covered an area 130 x 60 yards, making it four times larger than the Parthenon in Athens, Greece. The temple was originally built in the 8th century BC and dedicated to Artemis, a goddess in Greek mythology whom the Ephesians worshipped as a fertility idol. Destroyed by a flood in the 7th century BC, the temple was rebuilt, destroyed again in the 4th century BC, this time by an arsonist seeking vainglory, and then rebuilt again. By the 1st century AD, the Romans ruled Ephesus and had rebranded the Temple of Artemis as the Temple of Diana, a goddess in the Roman mythology. The substitution appears to have been fine with the local silversmiths as long as they could continue to peddle miniature shrines of Diana." (https://www.israeljerusalem.com/temple-of-diana-ephesus.htm)

Demetrius explains to the other workmen that not only was their trade of making idols for Diana in danger, but the very temple itself was in danger of being despised and her magnificence to be destroyed. He is afraid that Paul's preaching is going to turn men away from the worship of Diana completely. Verse 28 tells us that *"when they heard these sayings, they were full of wrath, and cried out, saying, Great is Diana of the Ephesians"*.

Acts 19:29 – 41 says, *"And the whole city was filled with confusion: and having caught Gaius and Aristarchus, men of Macedonia, Paul's companions in travel, they rushed with one accord into the theatre. 30 And when Paul would have entered in unto the people, the disciples suffered him not. 31 And certain of the chief of Asia, which were his friends, sent unto him, desiring him that he would not adventure himself into the theatre. 32 Some therefore cried one thing, and some another: for the assembly was confused; and the more part knew not wherefore they were come together. 33 And they drew Alexander out of the multitude, the Jews putting him forward. And Alexander beckoned with the hand, and would have made his defence unto the people. 34 But when they knew that he was a Jew, all with one voice about the space of two hours cried out, Great is Diana of the Ephesians. 35 And when the townclerk had appeased the people, he said, Ye men of Ephesus, what man is there that knoweth not how that the city of the Ephesians is a worshipper of the great goddess Diana, and of the image which fell down from Jupiter? 36 Seeing then that these things cannot be spoken against, ye ought to be quiet, and to do nothing rashly. 37 For ye have brought hither these men, which are neither robbers of churches, nor yet blasphemers of your goddess. 38 Wherefore if Demetrius, and the craftsmen which are with him, have a matter against any man, the law is open, and there are deputies: let them implead one another. 39 But if ye enquire any thing concerning other matters, it shall be determined in a lawful assembly. 40 For we are in danger to be called in question for this day's uproar, there being no cause whereby we may give an account of this concourse. 41 And when he had thus spoken, he dismissed the assembly."*

The city is in an uproar and they are filled with confusion. They then catch Gaius and Aristarchus who were Paul's companions in his travels, and rushed them into the theatre. They not doubt want to make a spectacle out of the men that have helped Paul so faithfully.

When Paul knows what is going on, he immediately tries to enter the theatre, but the disciples would not let him. Paul was going in to defend his brothers, but those he had led to the Lord there in Ephesus, would not allow him to go in. Others advised him that this was not a good idea, since the crowd was so stirred up, they would probably kill him.

The crowd was wild. The confusion was great. Some cried one thing and others cried something else. There was so much confusion. They could not agree. It was so bad that after a while they lost the real motive behind the riot. The largest part of the crowd did not even know why they were there. They didn't even know what the riot was all about.

We are told in verse 33 that the crowd drew Alexander out of the multitude and as he tried to make his defence they shut him down when they found out he was a Jew. Then the crowd began to cry out "Great is Diana of the Ephesians" for the next two hours.

Then the townclerk stepped forward to appease the people and then addresses them by telling them that everyone knows that the city of the Ephesians was a worshipper of the great goddess Diana. He tells them that everyone knows how that got started. Then he says that these things cannot be spoken against and because of that they should be quiet. He then tells them that if Paul and his laborers have violated the law, then they should take the proper channel to punish them. He is trying to tell these folk of Ephesus that rioting is not the answer. Allow the law to settle this problem.

In the closing words of this chapter, he urged the people to go home and then dismissed the crowd. It seems evident that he was successful in quieting this riot that had started in opposition to Paul and his laborers and their effective preaching in Ephesus.

PAUL GOES TO MACEDONIA

Acts 20: 1-5, "And after the uproar was ceased, Paul called unto him the disciples, and embraced them, and departed for to go into Macedonia. 2 And when he had gone over those parts, and had given them much exhortation, he came into Greece, 3 And there abode three months. And when the Jews laid wait for him, as he was about to sail into Syria, he purposed to return through Macedonia. 4 And there accompanied him into Asia Sopater of Berea; and of the Thessalonians, Aristarchus and Secundus; and Gaius of Derbe, and Timotheus; and of Asia, Tychicus and Trophimus. 5 These going before tarried for us at Troas."

After the riot has ended, then Paul calls the disciple in Ephesus and embraced them (showing they had a good fellowship), and said his goodbyes. Paul then departs into Macedonia. Through Macedonia he did much preaching and exhortation. Probably every place that Paul stopped he had a meeting.

Having passed through Macedonia, Paul now comes to Greece once again. Paul has preached here before and no doubt had a number of converts. One thing that is interesting about Paul is that when he comes to a place he calls out the believers and then preaches the Word of God to them. He does not try to entertain them, but desires to preach to them. That's what we need more of today. We don't need to be entertained or amused, be need preaching.

In verse three we are told that Paul stayed in Greece for about three months. Here he taught and exhorted the people from the Word of God and preached to them Christ. As he is about to sail into Syria, he finds out that the Jews were waiting for him to do him harm, so instead, he goes back to Macedonia. Here Paul preaches and exhorts the believers once again.

We are given a list in verse four of those that accompanied Paul into Asia. They are Sopater of Berea, this is probably the same Sosipater who is mentioned in Romans 16:21; Aristarchus and Secundus from Thessalonica; Gaius and Timotheus of Derbe; and of Asia, Tychicus and Trophimus. These went before Paul and tarried for him in Troas. Notice the verse says, "These going before tarried for us at Troas". The "us" here also indicates that Luke, the writer of the book of Acts, is with Paul at this time. These that are tarrying in Troas are waiting for Paul and Luke. Paul was no doubt preaching all along the way till he came to Troas.

Acts 20:6 – 12, "*And we sailed away from Philippi after the days of unleavened bread, and came unto them to Troas in five days; where we abode seven days. 7 And upon the first day of the week, when the disciples came together to break bread, Paul preached unto them, ready to depart on the morrow; and continued his speech until midnight. 8 And there were many lights in the upper chamber, where they were gathered together. 9 And there sat in a window a certain young man named Eutychus, being fallen into a deep sleep: and as Paul was long preaching, he sunk down with sleep, and fell down from the third loft, and was taken up dead. 10 And Paul went down, and fell on him, and embracing him said, Trouble not yourselves; for his life is in him. 11 When he therefore was come up again, and had broken bread, and eaten, and talked a long while, even till break of day, so he departed. 12 And they brought the young man alive, and were not a little comforted.*"

The "days of unleavened bread" are mentioned just to give us an idea of the time of year Paul was travelling. It

does not indicate that Paul kept or observed the Passover as
the Jews did. Matthew Henry tells us this was about the time
he had written in his first epistle to the church of Corinth,
and taught that Christ is our Passover, and a Christian life
and our feast of unleavened bread. In 1 Cor. 5: 7 and 8 it
says, "*Purge out therefore the old leaven, that ye may be a new
lump, as ye are unleavened. For even Christ our passover is
sacrificed for us: 8 Therefore let us keep the feast, not with old
leaven, neither with the leaven of malice and wickedness; but with
the unleavened bread of sincerity and truth.*" He is teaching
when the substance has come the shadow was done away.

Paul sails to them in Troas in five days and when he
arrives we are told he stays seven days. Paul traveled for
five days in order for the opportunity to preach here for
seven days. What a sacrifice just the time of travel was in
Paul's day! They had no modern means of transportation so
many of the miles were either made by walking, riding on a
donkey or on the sea by ship. How far are we willing to go
to get the gospel message out?

In verse seven we are told that it was on the first day of
the week when the disciples came together to break bread
that Paul preached to them. They prayed and sang psalms
and kept up their communion with God through the week,
but that was not enough for them. On the first day of the
week, Sunday, they gathered together to worship the Lord.
There should be stated times for Christians to come together.
They meet on the "Christian Sabbath" in honor of Christ, in
remembrance of His resurrection and Henry says, also the
pouring out of the Holy Spirit was on the first day of the
week. This was the believers practice to meet on this day for
worship. It surely ought to be our practice.

This was to be Paul's last day here and the Scripture tells
us that he "continued his speech until midnight". Have you

ever been in a service where there was preaching at midnight? I have and let me tell you the Spirit of God can still move at midnight just like He can on Sunday morning. In the average church today, most of the people would have already left and gone home. On Sunday morning, if the preacher goes past 12 noon, they are ready to mutiny and abandon ship. What's wrong with people?

We are told in verse 8 that they are meeting, not in a church building or a synagogue or a beautiful chapel or cathedral, but they are meeting in a house. The scripture tells us that there were many lights in the upper chamber where they were meeting. While Paul was long preaching, we are told of a young man by the name of Eutychus, who was sitting in one of the windows in the chamber and fell into a deep sleep. Verse 9 tells us that not only did he fall asleep, but he fell from the third loft, from the window in which he was sitting. He had gone into a deep sleep and as he fell we are told that he was taken up dead. The fall from the window while Paul was preaching had killed him.

Well, needless to say, this temporarily stopped the meeting. Paul and the congregation that was gathered there ran immediately to Eutychus. Paul lifted him in his arms and embraced him and told the believers "trouble not yourselves; for his life is in him." What a time they must have had in the yard of the house as this young man that had just been killed, was brought back to life. What a miracle! I'm sure there was some shouting and praising going on there that night. They may have even woke up a few people that had already gone to bed. What a testimony of the power of this man of God, the Apostle Paul!

With all of this happening you would think that the next thing would be to have the benediction and go home. But that's not what happened. They returned to the meeting room and broke bread and ate and then fellowshipped until the break of day. Not a lot of all-night prayer meetings going on anymore. Most people just don't have time for the preaching of the Word of God or the fellowship of the saints like they used to. Oh, how we need a revival through the land today!

As soon as it was day, Paul departed. The people left with the young man who was raised from the dead and verse 12 tells us that they *"were not a little comforted"*.

ON THE WAY TO JERUSALEM

Acts 20:13 – 16, "And we went before to ship, and sailed unto Assos, there intending to take in Paul: for so had he appointed, minding himself to go afoot. 14 And when he met with us at Assos, we took him in, and came to Mitylene. 15 And we sailed thence, and came the next day over against Chios; and the next day we arrived at Samos, and tarried at Trogyllium; and the next day we came to Miletus. 16 For Paul had determined to sail by Ephesus, because he would not spend the time in Asia: for he hasted, if it were possible for him, to be at Jerusalem the day of Pentecost."

Paul is still on his way to Jerusalem and now Luke says that they sailed by ship to Assos. Apparently, Paul had decided to go by foot. This may have been the shorter way, but still it was the hardest way. At Assos they met Paul and verse 14 tells us that they desired to take him in, meaning that they were going to bring him on board the ship. When they took Paul into the ship they sailed to Mitylene and the next day to Chios and the next day to Samos and they tarried at Trogyllium, then the next day sailed to Miletus. This was the sea port that lay near Ephesus. He had determined that he would not go to Ephesus at this time and so they sailed by Ephesus.

We are told in verse 16 that one reason he did not stop at Ephesus was because he was rushing to get to Jerusalem for the day of Pentecost. Paul's desire to be in Jerusalem at this time was so he could once again have the opportunity to preach the death, burial and resurrection of Jesus to the Jews there. It is evident from Paul's writings to the churches that many were trying to add the law to their salvation and that he was not going there to observe the Feast of Pentecost. I have been preaching from over fifty years and have never taken part in any of the Feast that the Jews were commanded to keep. It was a different dispensation. The Church Age brought in a new way of doing things. Christ had come and died and rose again that our sins might be forgiven and our faith in His finished work is all we need for salvation.

Paul had a burden for his people. Remember what he said in Romans 10:1 – 4, "*Brethren, my heart's desire and prayer to God for Israel is, that they might be saved. 2 For I bear them record that they have a zeal of God, but not according to knowledge. 3 For they being ignorant of God's righteousness, and going about to establish their own righteousness, have not submitted themselves unto the righteousness of God. 4 For Christ is the end of the law for righteousness to every one that believeth.*"

Paul was hastening to get to Jerusalem by the Feast of Pentecost because he wanted another opportunity to preach to the Jews about Jesus. He knew that if they could hear the message and believe the message that Christ would establish His righteousness in them.

Acts 20:17 – 25 say, "And from Miletus he sent to Ephesus, and called the elders of the church. 18 And when they were come to him, he said unto them, Ye know, from the first day that I came into Asia, after what manner I have been with you at all seasons, 19 Serving the Lord with all humility of mind, and with many tears, and temptations, which befell me by the lying in wait of the

Jews: 20 And how I kept back nothing that was profitable unto
you, but have shewed you, and have taught you publickly, and
from house to house, 21 Testifying both to the Jews, and also to the
Greeks, repentance toward God, and faith toward our Lord Jesus
Christ. 22 And now, behold, I go bound in the spirit unto
Jerusalem, not knowing the things that shall befall me there: 23
Save that the Holy Ghost witnesseth in every city, saying that
bonds and afflictions abide me. 24 But none of these things move
me, neither count I my life dear unto myself, so that I might finish
my course with joy, and the ministry, which I have received of the
Lord Jesus, to testify the gospel of the grace of God. 25 And now,
behold, I know that ye all, among whom I have gone preaching the
kingdom of God, shall see my face no more."

Though Paul did not choose to go to Ephesus, while he
was at Miletus he sent to Ephesus and called all the elders of
the church to come to him. Notice he did not call all the
congregation together, but rather the elders of the church.
From this passage at the end of chapter 20, it seems evident
that he was encouraging their hearts in the faith and also
seeking their prayers for him as he went to Jerusalem.

When they are gathered together Paul begins his speech.
He reminds them of what kind of man he was and is. He
reminds them that they knew from the first day that he came
what he taught and what he preached. The seasons did not
change him, nor what he believed. He tells them that he
served the Lord with all humility of mind, with many tears
and temptations which were brought on by the Jews
continually lying wait for him. He tells them that he has kept
back nothing that was profitable to them and that he taught
them edifying and encouraging them when he taught them
in their homes and in public meetings. His message had
been consistent. He did not waver. It never changed. He
preach repentance toward God and faith toward the Lord
Jesus Christ. We need to follow that example in our lives as

Christians. Don't waver from the faith in the Lord Jesus Christ.

Paul now gets to the hard part of the message. He tells them that he is going to Jerusalem, bound in the spirit. He knows that he must go but he does not know what will happen to him because of his teaching and preaching there. He tells them that the Holy Ghost has witnessed in the every city that bonds and afflictions are waiting for him. But then Paul makes the statement to these leaders in Ephesus that none of these things move me. Paul is determined to go no matter the cost even if it cost him his life. He declares to them that he wants to finish is course with joy. He wants to finish strong. He wants to complete the ministry that the Lord has put him in by preaching the gospel of the grace of God.

He tells them, probably the most disturbing news they have heard, that they shall see his face no more. This is disturbing news to these believers because they loved Paul. It was Paul that had told them about Jesus. It was Paul that had persuaded them to receive the Lord Jesus Christ into their lives. It was Paul that had faithfully taught them the Word of the Lord. Now he tells them that this is the last time you will see me. I won't be visiting you anymore. I won't be teaching you anymore. Today is the last time you will see my face. How that must have crushed these believer's that loved him so.

PAUL'S FINAL WORDS TO EPHESUS

Acts 20:26 – 38 says, *"Wherefore I take you to record this day, that I am pure from the blood of all men. 27 For I have not shunned to declare unto you all the counsel of God. 28 Take heed therefore unto yourselves, and to all the flock, over the which the Holy Ghost hath made you overseers, to feed the church of God, which he hath purchased with his own blood. 29 For I know this, that after my departing shall grievous wolves enter in among you, not sparing the flock. 30 Also of your own selves shall men arise, speaking perverse things, to draw away disciples after them. 31 Therefore watch, and remember, that by the space of three years I ceased not to warn every one night and day with tears. 32 And now, brethren, I commend you to God, and to the word of his grace, which is able to build you up, and to give you an inheritance among all them which are sanctified. 33 I have coveted no man's silver, or gold, or apparel. 34 Yea, ye yourselves know, that these hands have ministered unto my necessities, and to them that were with me. 35 I have shewed you all things, how that so labouring ye ought to support the weak, and to remember the words of the Lord Jesus, how he said, It is more blessed to give than to receive. 36 And when he had thus spoken, he kneeled down, and prayed with them all. 37 And they all wept sore, and fell on Paul's neck, and kissed him, 38 Sorrowing most of all for the words which he spake, that they should see his face no more. And they accompanied him unto the ship."*

Paul continues his speech by stating that he is pure from the blood of all me. What a statement! In Romans 1:15 – 16 he says, *"So, as much as in me is, I am ready to preach the gospel to you that are at Rome also. 16 For I am not ashamed of the gospel of Christ: for it is the power of God unto salvation to every one that believeth; to the Jew first, and also to the Greek."*

Paul says three things in Romans 1 that shows his faithfulness to tell all men about Jesus. First of all he says *"I am a debtor"*. Paul uses this phrase three times. Then he says, *"I am ready"*, and then *"I am not ashamed"*. Paul has spent 20 to 25 years preaching and teaching the Word of God in Asia Minor and on the continent of Europe and he is telling them that no one can point a finger at me and tell me I never told them about Christ.

Every time we fail to be a witness for our Lord, we have their blood on our hands. Dr. Sightler said "In other words, you have failed to be a witness, you have failed to give your testimony, you have failed in faithful service and devotion to the Lord. And as a result, somebody might have stumbled over your apathy and over your neglect into Hell without God and without hope." What a sad picture, but Paul said I am pure from the blood of all men. Have you done all you could to reach lost souls for Christ?

Paul tells them that he has preached to them the whole counsel of God. Matthew Henry says, "The gospel is the counsel of God; it is admirably contrived by his wisdom, it is unalterably determined by his will, and it is kindly designed by his grace for our glory."

1 Corinthians 2:1 – 7 says, "*And I, brethren, when I came to you, came not with excellency of speech or of wisdom, declaring unto you the testimony of God. 2 For I determined not to know any thing among you, save Jesus Christ, and him crucified. 3 And I was with you in weakness, and in fear, and in much trembling. 4 And my speech and my preaching was not with enticing words of man's wisdom, but in demonstration of the Spirit and of power: 5 That your faith should not stand in the wisdom of men, but in the power of God. 6 Howbeit we speak wisdom among them that are perfect: yet not the wisdom of this world, nor of the princes of this world, that come to nought: 7 But we speak the wisdom of God in a mystery, even the hidden wisdom, which God ordained before the world unto our glory:*"

Another good reason to always use the King James Version of the Word of God in your study, your teaching and your preaching. (Refer to my book on "God's Precious Word" page 39-41.) The modern versions of the Bible do not contain the whole counsel of God. There are verses that are changed and many that are left out altogether. Some say

"Oh, but the "other versions" are easier to read. In her book, "The Language of the King James Bible", Mrs. Gail Riplinger continuing her research in the readability of the King James Bible says, "Recent evaluation shows the reading level of the King James Bible to be fifth grade, as a whole—many individual passages would be lower. The modern Bibles are shown to be between sixth and ninth grade levels as a whole. The modern versions claim to increase readability when in reality, they often make readability more difficult. Stick with the preserved Word of God.

Paul charges these elders to be diligent and faithful in the work that the Lord has called them to do. He places the government of the church in their hands. He begins with the words, "take heed". First to themselves and then to the church. If you are not right with God and living a dedicated life to Him, then no one else is going to want to hear what you have to say. He reminds them that the Holy Ghost has made them overseers of the church and their duty is to feed them. "Overseer" means a guardian or bishop. Many churches are starving to death because they are not being fed. Oh, how the ministers of God need to heed this charge today and began feeding the flock with the Word of God. He also reminds them that the church they are charged with has been "purchased with his own blood". Thank God, the believer belongs to the Lord!

They need to be feeding the flock every chance they get because Paul then gives a disturbing statement. He said, *"that after my departing shall grievous wolves enter in among you, not sparing the flock"*. Paul is address those who knew well his persecution. Paul is reminding them that even after he is gone, those who persecute will still be present. He is referring to the false teachers that shall come and though they may be in sheep's clothing, they are grievous wolves. This false teachers will come in among them and try to deceive them from the truth. They will sow discord among the brethren. They will try to draw them away from the pure gospel of Christ. They will seek to defame those who hold to the truth. In Philippians 3:2 Paul refers to these this way, *"Beware of dogs, beware of evil workers, beware of the concision."*

In verse 30 he tells them that even those in the church will rise up and speak perverse things and draw away many disciples. These "perverse things" are things spoken contrary to the right rule of the gospel. Their intent is destructive. They are not trying to build a church, but rather tear one down. In Peter's second epistle, in chapter 3 and in verse 16 he mentions those this was, *"As also in all his epistles, speaking in them of these things; in which are some things hard to be understood, which they that are unlearned and unstable wrest, as they do also the other scriptures, unto their own destruction."* Hymenaeus and Philetus are examples in 2 Timothy 2:17 - 18, *"And their word will eat as doth a canker: of whom is Hymenaeus and Philetus; 18 Who concerning the truth have erred, saying that the resurrection is past already; and overthrow the faith of some."*

He admonishes them to "watch". Then he gives the example of himself and tells them to remember that he ceased not for three years to warn everyone night and day and he did it with tears. Compassion for and concern about the congregation will go a long way. Paul was a forceful preacher wherever he went but he sowed the seed with his tears. He is telling these church leaders as Dr. Sightler put it "to build upon the foundation I put down, and while you build, you watch for these grievous wolves." Watch for these men for they will arise.

Paul finishes his speech here beginning in verse 32 where he commends them to God and to the word of his grace, which is the word of Christ's grace. He tells them that this word will edify others, *"which is able to build you up"*. He also tells them that it will glorify them, *"to give you an inheritance among all them which are sanctified"*. Commend means to place them into God's hands. Since they were not going to be able to see Paul again after he departed, Paul commends them unto God, for he knows that God can help them through their struggles of life.

Paul sets himself up as an example of how they should live before the people. He says that he has not coveted other men's silver or gold or apparel. Paul was not in the ministry for the money, but for the winning of the lost to Christ and for their edification. Paul reminds them what they already know, that he worked for what he needed and for the needs of those laboring with him. He reminds them that he taught them, both with his mouth and by example, to labor to help support the weak, and to remember the words that Jesus said, "It is more blessed to give than to receive."

When Paul had ended his speech, we are told that he kneeled down and prayed with them. Their response was that they wept sore and fell on Paul's neck and kissed him. There can be no doubt of the love that they had for this man of God. Their greatest sorrow was that Paul had told them that they should see his face no more. These all followed him down to the ship and watched as Paul left on his journey to Jerusalem.

PAUL ARRIVES AT JERUSALEM

Acts 21:1 – 17, *"And it came to pass, that after we were gotten from them, and had launched, we came with a straight course unto Coos, and the day following unto Rhodes, and from thence unto Patara: 2 And finding a ship sailing over unto Phenicia, we went aboard, and set forth.*

3 *Now when we had discovered Cyprus, we left it on the left hand, and sailed into Syria, and landed at Tyre: for there the ship was to unlade her burden. 4 And finding disciples, we tarried there seven days: who said to Paul through the Spirit, that he should not go up to Jerusalem.*

5 *And when we had accomplished those days, we departed and went our way; and they all brought us on our way, with wives and children, till we were out of the city: and we kneeled down on the shore, and prayed. 6 And when we had taken our leave one of another, we took ship; and they returned home again. 7 And when we had finished our course from Tyre, we came to Ptolemais, and saluted the brethren, and abode with them one day. 8 And the next day we that were of Paul's company departed, and came unto Caesarea: and we entered into the house of Philip the evangelist, which was one of the seven; and abode with him. 9 And the same man had four daughters, virgins, which did prophesy. 10 And as we tarried there many days, there came down from Judaea a certain prophet, named Agabus. 11 And when he was come unto us, he took Paul's girdle, and bound his own hands and feet, and said, Thus saith the Holy Ghost, So shall the Jews at Jerusalem bind the man that owneth this girdle, and shall deliver him into the hands of the Gentiles. 12 And when we heard these things, both we, and they of that place, besought him not to go up to Jerusalem. 13 Then Paul answered, What mean ye to weep and to break mine heart? for I am ready not to be bound only, but also to die at Jerusalem for the name of the Lord Jesus. 14 And when he would not be persuaded, we ceased, saying, The will of the Lord be done. 15 And after those days we took up our carriages, and went up to Jerusalem. 16 There went with us also certain of the disciples of Caesarea, and brought with them one Mnason of Cyprus, an old disciple, with whom we should lodge. 17 And when we were come to Jerusalem, the brethren received us gladly."*

When Paul had sailed from Miletus they came on a straight course to Coos and the next day to Rhodes and then to Patara. There they found a ship going to Phenicia and got on board. They sailed past Cyprus and sailed into Syria and landed at Tyre. We are told that here the ship was to be unloaded of its cargo. Paul immediately found disciples here and saw a great opportunity to teach them and remained seven days. They urged Paul through the Spirit not to go to Jerusalem. When those seven days were over they followed Paul and his companions down to the shore where Luke says that they prayed. From Tyre they came to Ptolemais and spent one day saluting the brethren. The next day Paul and his company came to Caesarea and stayed at the house of Philip the evangelist.

This is the same Philip that we saw in Acts 8. Dr. Sightler says that it is an interesting insight that Philip, the evangelist who conducted the great revival in Samaria, when he had to leave it and go win the Ethiopian eunuch to God in Acts 8, is still busy serving the Lord, having his family in subjection and witnessing and preaching in the city of Caesarea in the land of Israel. Here Paul and Luke and those with him spend some days at his house.

In verse 9 we are told that Philip had four daughters that were virgins and they did prophecy. Dr. Sightler says about this that "There are some naïve people who suggest because of the expression "which did prophesy" that these four daughters were women preachers. I say to you the word "prophesy" does not necessarily mean to preach the Word of God or to assume the lordship of a congregation of people. As far as I am concerned, God does not call women to preach, and I would not recommend a woman as pastor. . . . The word "prophesy" in verse 9, literally means or actually means that these four young ladies gave a vivid testimony from their own heart of the grace of God. They so lived close to the Lord that they could stand up and declare a good testimony. And the word "prophesy" means to give witness in jubilance and in joy and in spiritual ecstasy. To make the word "prophesy" mean that these young ladies were women preachers is stretching the Scripture more than is wise to do so. . . . These daughters of Philip were not women preachers, not by any means, but they were testifying and witnessing young ladies who bore a good testimony in their community to the resurrection of Jesus Christ from the dead." ("Acts" Dr. Harold B. Sightler, page 317 and 318) I feel the main purpose of this being here is to show us that Philip was faithful in preaching Jesus to his family as well as to others.

As they tarried there many days we are told that Agabus, a certain prophet from Judea came down. He came with a message for Paul. When he came to them he took Paul's girdle and bound his hands and feet. He then told him that the Holy Ghost said that the man who owns this girdle will be bound by the Jews and they will deliver him into the hands of the Jews. Another warning for Paul not to go to Jerusalem. When they heard this message they all began to try to get Paul not to go to Jerusalem.

Paul's response was why are you weeping and breaking my heart? He tells them that he is ready not only to be bound in Jerusalem, but to die there for the name of the Lord Jesus Christ. Paul was determined that this was what he had to do. He driving passion and love for his people pushed him on. He would not be persuaded to give up this thing he knew he must do. When the people saw that they could not change his mind, they stopped trying and simply said "*the will of the Lord be done*".

In verse 15 they took up their carriages (baggage or luggage) and went up to Jerusalem. There were certain disciples from Caesarea that went with them. These also brought an old man from Cyprus with them by the name of Mnason "*with whom we should lodge*". It would seem that Mnason had a home in Jerusalem that they all stayed in while there during the Feast of Pentecost.

110

Verse 17 tells us that when they arrived in Jerusalem the brethren received us gladly. Many of the believers and disciples were in Jerusalem and were so excited to see Paul and his companions as they have returned from their long mission trip. Thus ends the third missionary journey of Paul.

A summary of what Paul faced is given in 2 Corinthians 11:23-31, "*Are they ministers of Christ? (I speak as a fool) I am more; in labours more abundant, in stripes above measure, in prisons more frequent, in deaths oft. 24 Of the Jews five times received I forty stripes save one. 25 Thrice was I beaten with rods, once was I stoned, thrice I suffered shipwreck, a night and a day I have been in the deep; 26 In journeyings often, in perils of waters, in perils of robbers, in perils by mine own countrymen, in perils by the heathen, in perils in the city, in perils in the wilderness, in perils in the sea, in perils among false brethren; 27 In weariness and painfulness, in watchings often, in hunger and thirst, in fastings often, in cold and nakedness. 28 Beside those things that are without, that which cometh upon me daily, the care of all the churches. 29 Who is weak, and I am not weak? who is offended, and I burn not? 30 If I must needs glory, I will glory of the things which concern mine infirmities. 31 The God and Father of our Lord Jesus Christ, which is blessed for evermore, knoweth that I lie not.*"

How Can We Support and Send Out Missionaries?

I believe that missions is the heart beat of God. Therefore, missions should be one of the primary interest of the church. God will always bless a mission minded church. I saw that from pastoring for over 25 years. We were able, by faith, to support more missionaries than we had people coming to church. What a blessing to support missionaries that you know personally. There's actually a thrill of being able to know that missionary and his family and know that when they win a soul on the mission field, God will put that on our account, because we had helped send that missionary to preach the gospel.

I have found in my years as a pastor that the best way to introduce your church to missions is to allow them to see firsthand what a missionary does. We did this by having a missionary and his family come by the church and give a testimony, preach or show slides and tell about what it is like on the mission field winning souls to Jesus.

The best way to support missionaries is to be able to know the missionary and what they are doing or planning to do on the mission field. We had many come by the church and myself and the church became great friends and supporters of many of these missionaries through the years. To be able to know where your money is going and what it is doing for the cause of Christ is priceless.

Many churches across the country today use what is called Faith Promise Missions. It is a simple to understand program to support missions and missionaries that really works. Some attribute the beginning of Faith Promise

Missions to Dr. A. B. Simpson. He claimed to have gotten it from the Bible. I agree!

Faith in dealing with our finances is just as important as having faith and applying it in any other area of our lives. If we give by faith, God will provide what we need in a marvelous way, both in giving to missions and in having what we need supplied along the way.

We will never be able to do a great work for the Lord without faith! In 2 Corinthians 10:15-16 says, *"Not boasting of things without our measure, that is, of other men's labours; but having hope, when your faith is increased, that we shall be enlarged by you according to our rule abundantly, To preach the gospel in the regions beyond you, and not to boast in another man's line of things made ready to our hand."*

Notice he tells us that "When your faith is increased" then "we shall be enlarged by you," the purpose, "to preach the gospel in the regions beyond you". What a picture of faith promise missions we see in these verses. They show us that as our faith increases, we will give more and that will cause the missionary to be supported to the place they can reach the field and even to the regions beyond.

In 2 Corinthians chapters 8 and 9, we see at least 8 Biblical principles that define faith promise mission giving. The first thing we must do if we are to be faithful, fruitful givers to faith promise missions is in verse 5, we must first give ourselves to the Lord.

This is the most important of all the principles we see in these two chapters. If we don't belong to the Lord, nothing we do is going to prosper. If we belong to him and have not given ourselves to him to use in His service, then we are not ready to give our money. We must be willing to give ourselves or we will never be willing to give our money!

2 Corinthians 8:5 says, "And this they did, not as we hoped, but first gave their own selves to the Lord, and unto us by the will of God."

How important it is that before we undertake a program for giving to missions, we first examine ourselves and see where we stand. Then completely and totally commit ourselves to the Lord. If we have yielding all of ourselves to Him, then we are ready to invest all that the Lord would have us to in giving to missions. Search your heart! What is your commitment level to the Lord today! He doesn't want part of you, He wants all of you! Give Him your all today!

The second principle that we must meet in our faith promise giving is in 2 Corinthians 9:6, 7, "But this I say, He which soweth sparingly shall reap also sparingly; and he which soweth bountifully shall reap also bountifully. Every man according as he purposeth in his heart, so let him give; not grudgingly, or of necessity: for God loveth a cheerful giver."

Our attitude concerning our giving must be cheerful. The way we give, whether sparingly or bountiful, demonstrates our desire to further the work of God.
2 Corinthians 8:3 says, "For to their power, I bear record, yea, and beyond their power, they were willing of themselves."

2 Corinthians 8:12 says, "For if there be first a willing mind, it is accepted according to that a man hath, and not according to that he hath not."

We must give out of our willingness to give and not out of duty. We must have a willing mind in giving and that will lead to a willing heart. We give because we want to see the work of the Lord continue and prosper. We give because we want to see souls saved and then discipled through the teaching of the Word of God. We give because we care about others and are willing to give to try to reach them and help them in the Lord.

In verse 2 of 2 Corinthians 8 we are told, *"How in a great trial of affliction the abundance of their joy and their deep poverty abounded unto the riches of their liberality."* Their giving by faith allowed them to give "beyond their power". We are to give out of our need rather than out of our excess. This is real sacrificial giving!

It is emphasized that every believer should be involved in giving by faith.
2 Corinthians 8: 7 says, *"Therefore, as ye abound in every thing, in faith, and utterance, and knowledge, and in all diligence, and in your love to us, see that ye abound in this grace also."* Paul show us in these two chapters that financing missions does not depend on having a lot of money, but on having a willing heart.

2 Cor. 8:1-7 1. *Moreover, brethren, we do you to wit of the grace of God bestowed on the churches of Macedonia; 2 How that in a great trial of affliction the abundance of their joy and their deep poverty abounded unto the riches of their liberality. 3 For to their power, I bear record, yea, and beyond their power they were willing of themselves; 4 Praying us with much intreaty that we would receive the gift, and take upon us the fellowship of the ministering to the saints. 5 And this they did, not as we hoped, but first gave their own selves to the Lord, and unto us by the will of God. 6 Insomuch that we desired Titus, that as he had begun, so he would also finish in you the same grace also. 7 Therefore, as ye abound in every thing, in faith, and utterance, and knowledge, and in all diligence, and in your love to us, see that ye abound in this grace also."*

Faith Promise Giving is an offering that is over and above your local church support. It is a promise, by faith, to contribute a certain amount over a period of a year. It was given by faith. God will honor a "faith commitment" of a Christian by making His grace abound. Grace usually comes in one of three ways. 1. New opportunities, such as overtime, new job, extra job. 2. Discipline, meaning a change in your life-style. 3. Grace of Unusual circumstances, such as in response to prayer, God answers in an unexpected way.

Faith Promise Giving allows the Lord an opportunity to work in our lives to give to reach the lost.
Faith Promise Giving says, "by faith, I will give $ _____ each week, or month to the Lord for missionary work".
Faith Promise Giving is a means of us fulfilling the great commission.
Faith Promise Giving is a means of weekly consistent discipline on our part to support World Missions.
Faith Promise Giving is an extra gift that you would not be able to give apart from trusting God to provide it.

Paul teaches us in 2 Cor. 8 and 9 that Faith Promise giving is (8:2-4) going to be more than you can afford. It will follow a personal commitment of giving yourself to the Lord, (8:5). It is not a commandment, but a commitment (8:8). It is something that is previously promised (9:5). It is something you personally purpose to give (9:7). It is a gift that you can give cheerfully (9:7). It is a gift, by faith, that God will provide (9:8).

How can you get involved? I have listed a few things here that will help you.

First, you need to realize that, as a Christian, God has entrusted you with the Gospel message, (1 Thess. 2:4, *"But as we were allowed of God to be put in trust with the gospel, even so*

we speak; not as pleasing men, but God, which trieth our hearts."
Secondly, we are commanded to take this Gospel to those
around us and into all the world, (Acts 1:8, *"But ye shall
receive power, after that the Holy Ghost is come upon you: and ye
shall be witnesses unto me both in Jerusalem, and in all Judea, and
in Samaria, and unto the uttermost part of the earth."*

Pray about what God would have you to give and be
faithful to give that on a regular basis. See how God will
bless you in being involved in world missions and enjoy the
blessing of giving to get the message of the Gospel to a lost
and dying world. Why not pray about getting involved in
Faith Promise Giving today?

54011867R00068